René&me

René&me

AN AUTOBIOGRAPHY

Gorden Kaye

with Hilary Bonner

SIDGWICK & JACKSON
LONDON

Acknowledgements

*To the dozens of cousins and to all the fans for
their love and support. And to Jeremy
Lloyd and David Croft OBE, without
whom etc., etc. . . .*

First published in Great Britain in 1989
by Sidgwick & Jackson Limited
1 Tavistock Chambers, Bloomsbury Way
London WC1A 2SG

ISBN 0 283 99965 9

Photoset in Linotron Sabon by
Rowland Phototypesetting Limited
Bury St Edmunds, Suffolk
Printed in Great Britain by
Mackays of Chatham plc, Chatham, Kent

Contents

To my dear mother
Gracie, who left too soon.

GORDEN KAYE

Before We Start

Introduction by Hilary Bonner

This is the story of a lovely, witty, talented, single-minded, sometimes difficult and sometimes tormented man. Gorden Kaye is a television hero who dislikes being called a star. 'Stars are people like Frank Sinatra and James Stewart and Paul Newman,' he says. 'I am not a star.' Yet to the millions who love him as René in *'Allo 'Allo*, that is exactly what he is. And this is Gorden's life story written in his own words, charting the path that has taken him from a terraced house in Huddersfield to Café René somewhere in wartime France. He tells it like it is and he tells only the truth.

Gorden Kaye and I were neighbours whose paths had crossed several times professionally before we embarked on this project. And we spent many hours together unravelling his past. Sometimes we sat in the living room of my house overlooking the river in West London, and sometimes in his just down the road. Over coffee and orange juice and Perrier water and tea – never anything stronger because Gorden doesn't much like alcohol – we talked on occasions deep into the night.

When I first suggested to Gorden that we should write this book his initial reaction was to say no. He feared that what I had in mind was merely a more detailed revelation of aspects of his personal life which had become public knowledge in early 1989.

I told him that I wanted simply to help him tell the story of his life, the ups and downs, the laughter and the tears, the thrills and the spills, the good moments and the bad. I told him that I believed his sexuality was just a part of him, and should be treated as such in the book – that I wanted to know about his family and his boyhood, his schooldays, his first jobs and his first loves, his early days in the theatre, his time on *Coronation Street* and his years working as a jobbing actor with some of the most famous and colourful people in showbusiness.

Gorden looked a little puzzled. 'But who would be interested in all that? Who would be interested in my life story?' he asked.

He is the star of a TV show which pulls in 16 million viewers regularly, and of a stage show which has smashed West End theatre records left, right and centre. But he meant it. There are still moments when he cannot really believe the huge appeal of *'Allo 'Allo* and all that has happened because of it – his fame, his increasing fortune, his popularity as an after-dinner speaker and as a celebrity constantly in demand for public appearances, his acceptance even on the fringe of royal circles and his membership of the hallowed showbiz charity society, the Water Rats.

He remains the only son of Harold and Gracie Kaye of Huddersfield, brought up on a diet of common sense and survival, of living close to the poverty line but always keeping a best suit for Sundays. And it was in these early years that the character of Gorden Kaye, the television personality, was fashioned. I hope the chapters about Gorden's childhood, the solid working-class Yorkshire family he was born into, his close relationship with his mother and father, and his youth spent working in industry will help illustrate the kind of man he is.

He has relived in these pages the painful awkwardness of his youth and his dreadful shyness. And how the uncertain, overweight office boy was transformed when he became an amateur radio disc jockey and joined a drama group. Of his stage début he says: 'It was a kind of homecoming.' He is reluctant to give that moment in his life too much importance in case it is difficult to believe, or sounds silly. To me it has always sounded quite simply like the truth.

Three years ago, by sheer coincidence, I sat next to Gorden at the annual Television and Radio Industries Club awards when *'Allo 'Allo* had been voted Best BBC Comedy for the first time in

1986. There was some confusion over who should collect the award. In between the main course and the pudding David Croft – *'Allo 'Allo*'s producer and co-writer – asked Gorden if he would go up.

A little startled – this was a big gathering of important people in front of TV cameras, and a bit more notice is normally given – Gorden proceeded to scribble a few notes on his table napkin. Then, without reference to those notes, he gave us two minutes of perfectly timed René – and brought the house down.

The next year *'Allo 'Allo* won again, and Gorden and his screen wife Carmen Silvera collected the trophy together. The following year *'Allo 'Allo* was not chosen. *Bread* won the Best Comedy award and Gorden was called upon to present it. As René he told the audience: 'Being asked to present this award really means something. It means we 'ave not won it, for a start.'

I recently went to the first recording of the latest series of *'Allo 'Allo* at the BBC TV Centre, and sat among the studio audience as Gorden treated them not only to his usual smashing performance but also to a warm-up comedy act. It is not often that the star of the show plays stand-up comic like that. Gorden seems to do so with ease – and he writes his own lines too. As he began his warm-up act two girls arrived late and were shown to their seats.

'Where are you from?' asked René.

'From Italy,' came the reply.

'Oh, that's not bad,' said René. 'Good excuse for being late, I suppose.'

His professionalism is total. He is a natural who has worked hard to hone the talent he was lucky enough to be born with. David Croft wanted to make Gorden the central character in a sitcom from the moment he first worked with him. 'I recognized him as a great comic talent,' says David. But he does not hesitate when you ask him what Gorden Kaye's greatest fault is. 'He does like to get it right,' he says with a chuckle.

In this book Gorden Kaye explains how he uses René Artois as somebody to hide behind. I believe, in fact, that throughout his adult life he has used the theatre as a welcome escape from the harsher aspects of bleak reality. Because of this he is not an easy man to get to know. That is not deliberate – and we have both worked hard in this book to reveal the real Gorden Kaye. It has been a surprisingly complex but, I think, worthwhile task.

With integrity and honesty Gorden has decided to talk openly about his sexuality. And this was not easy for him. Sex and love are not easy subjects for most of us to discuss, particularly if we are British. And for many, homosexual love is beyond comprehension. I remember when Gorden and I sat and talked about these delicate matters. When he is being serious Gorden speaks quietly and very precisely. He expresses his beliefs with care and sincerity.

In spite of his own protestations that he does not feel particularly intelligent he is a very bright man, a good talker and a great story-teller. Above all, he has the ability to make others laugh. Yet this is a man who has told me that he feels out of his depth in smart restaurants and chooses to avoid them whenever possible. Strange to reflect that most posh restaurants would probably form a queue to have him as a customer and would make a huge fuss of him. That, of course, would embarrass him even more. The working-class lad still lurks there somewhere. In *'Allo 'Allo* Gorden has achieved a unique comedy creation. And in these pages the man behind René is revealed for the first time.

Hilary Bonner
London
July 1989

Chapter One

How 'René' Came Alive

The big brown envelope dropped through the letter box, but it never reached the wall-to-wall special offer carpet. I was sitting anxiously behind the door waiting to catch it.

They had told me to expect a very funny script for a new TV comedy series. I pounced upon it eagerly and ripped it open. The first thing that fell out at my feet was a letter from the writer, David Croft, asking me to read the enclosed with a view to playing the part of 'René' in a thing called 'Allo 'Allo.

I read it as Renée, the girl's name. With that awful long hard E in the middle. I was absolutely horrified. I thought, oh my God it's about the backstage goings on of a drag artist. No, not even for David can I come up with that.

I had already worked for David Croft and admired him tremendously as the creator of quite brilliant sitcoms like *Dad's Army, It Ain't Half Hot Mum, Are You Being Served?* and *Hi-De-Hi*. But my first reaction was that this time he was about to make an extremely embarrassing mistake. So it was with grave misgivings, and some time later that I made myself a cup of tea, lit the inevitable cigarette, sat down in my favourite armchair, put my feet up, and began to study the script for the pilot episode of the TV show which was to transform my life.

I quickly realized that thankfully I had got entirely the wrong idea. There was this hilarious script about the most unlikely of subjects, the Nazi occupation of France.

Within minutes I was laughing aloud. Almost instantly I decided this was for me – I just had to do it. Whatever happened, I had to give it a go. David Croft has said publicly that he wrote *'Allo 'Allo* for me. And as I sat in that armchair that fateful day I could feel the character of René coming alive inside my head. I could hear his speech, I could see him in action.

People often ask me now if I thought in the beginning that *'Allo 'Allo* would be such a huge success, and the honest answer is that, yes, I could visualize the possibilities stretching endlessly ahead as soon as I studied that script. I suppose I did not imagine it becoming quite as enormous as it has worldwide – who could? – but I knew it was special.

I loved René from the start. He was obviously the pivot to the whole thing. This cowardly, cunning, randy man who makes you laugh at things you shouldn't. He always says what he thinks. He's eternally truthful.

I think for me the moment that best sums up René's character was when he was captured and was going to be shot by a firing squad. Yvette, his waitress girlfriend played by Vicki Michelle, goes to visit him in jail and tells him emotionally: 'When you die I will be at your side.'

René is unimpressed. He replies: 'If you stood in front of me I would 'ave a better chance.'

Well, that is the truth, isn't it? And it's typical René – direct, honest and funny in a way he really ought not to be.

René makes me laugh every time. And I've always thought that is a good start for an actor playing a comedy role. There's only been one bad moment really, and that was at the first rehearsals.

David Croft had got together this big cast of fourteen or fifteen people, and we gathered one sunny September morning in 1982 at the BBC's North Acton rehearsal rooms to read through this wonderful document that we all thought was the funniest thing we'd ever seen. We started to read and there was a silence. Quite a loud silence. One or two titters escaped unnoticed – but nothing stronger. We all thought, oh my God, have we made a mistake in saying yes? Are we kidding ourselves? Perhaps this is not quite as funny as we think it is after all.

Anyway we chatted among ourselves. Carmen Silvera had been chosen as René's wife, partly at my suggestion. We were already beginning a friendship that was to become an important part of my life. I remember talking to Carmen and saying, it will be all right, you know, David knows what he is doing. He'll make it come together, I'm sure of it. The truth was that, for just that brief moment, I wasn't sure at all.

We had nine or ten days of rehearsal before we had to record, and at first none of us were specially happy. Then as the days passed we began to click, and it did indeed come together.

I think we just had starting nerves. We were faced with this blank wall we were about to climb over and we didn't really know what was on the other side. *'Allo 'Allo* was different. I sometimes think we owe quite a thank you to whoever it was at the BBC who did not throw David Croft out when he first offered up the idea. After all, what the Nazis did in France during the war is not something that is normally joked about – and yet now, incredibly, the series is so widely accepted that it is even shown on French television.

We did take a fair bit of flak to begin with from people who felt we had no right to take that time and that situation in that location and turn it into something humorous. I am sure there are those who still feel we are wrong. But the majority, 16 million viewers per episode in this country alone, seem to understand what we are doing and can laugh at us without a problem.

In the early days *'Allo 'Allo* was a rather curious unknown quantity and we were under a great deal of pressure to get it right. We actors used to hurtle across the rehearsal room between scenes just to keep the buzz going. To make it flow.

But quite quickly something happened then that still happens now after all these episodes. Instead of people drifting off into a corner after they have finished their scene – which is usual – they will stay and watch the next scene and act as an audience to the artists who are working. They will be trying things out, bouncing things off you, laughing – or not laughing – which can tell you quite a lot. We are our best and most critical audience.

And there have been some hilarious moments. When Arthur

Bostrom, who plays Crabtree the gendarme with the appalling French accent, made his first appearance in the programme he was supposed to be dropped by parachute, and we were to find him hanging from a tree in which his harness had become entangled. The two waitresses had to climb on to my back and release him. The idea was that one of the waitresses would start to fall, grab at Arthur to save herself, and that she would then pull his trousers off and we would all land in a crumpled heap on the ground, leaving Arthur dangling in his Y-fronts.

Well, in the first take she got hold of not only his trousers but everything else as well, including his underpants, and left poor Arthur dangling in more ways than one, naked from the waist down. Somewhere in the BBC film library there remains a shot of Arthur Bostrom in this compromising position.

On another occasion on location – Carmen Silvera talked about this on my *This Is Your Life* because it is still a matter of some concern to her – the two British airmen were disguised as a pantomime cow. In order to conceal them and at the same time move them from one place to the other we put them amongst a bunch of real black and white cows. Meanwhile René and Edith were lurking behind a hedge. All went well until the cows decided that our hedge was the perfect place for them to answer their various calls of nature. Carmen and I were trapped between a barbed wire fence and all these cows relieving themselves. The danger was considerable, the cameras were rolling, and the crew and the rest of the cast were loving every moment of it.

In the same episode our two airmen in their cow outfit ultimately made their getaway on a tandem bicycle and Herr Flick's car was blown up. As so often happens during filming we had to act our reaction to the explosion before the stunt was staged. Somebody shouted 'Bang' and we obligingly threw ourselves to the floor. Then an explosion was actually staged and it was like an Exocet missile. We practically jumped out of our skins – much more so than when we had been acting.

We all enjoy those kind of incidents, particularly when somebody else is at the butt of them, but I am afraid the *'Allo 'Allo* team is something of a mutual admiration society. That, really, is the way it has been since the beginning. We reckoned the programme was good and that we could all be good in it.

The rewards came early. The night we recorded the pilot the studio audience were on the ceiling. We all knew we were starting a great adventure and the atmosphere was quite electric. I have rarely been so excited. We did the show on a Saturday night in Studio Eight at the BBC TV Centre, and on the Monday morning I heard through the grapevine that there was a buzz going around that they had found a new sitcom that was going to rule the world.

The extraordinary thing was that because of David Croft's previous commitments it was over a year before we made another *'Allo 'Allo*. He was a very busy man, still doing *Hi-De-Hi!* and *It Ain't Half Hot Mum*, and 1983 was just an empty year for us.

So life carried on much as before. In spite of that moment when the adrenalin flowed I was still Gorden Kaye the character actor from Huddersfield, almost always in work, doing quite nicely thank you, but largely unrecognized.

That was not to last. René lurked just around the corner. He was to take me with him into a whole new world that a working-class Yorkshire lad could not have dreamed of. Now I have to get used to being recognized everywhere I go, and on the days when I would much rather be anonymous there is little I can do about it. Disguises do not work with me. René's face is my face. Even the moustache is my own. John Inman, as Mr Humphries in *Are You Being Served?*, once suggested to me that I wear a hat. Hopeless. I just look like René in a hat. Sunglasses don't help either. Then I am René in sunglasses.

Four years ago I went to Northern Ireland with the National Theatre Company and we played *Animal Farm* in Belfast. A few of us went sight-seeing one day and were trying to find the famous Giant's Causeway. We took the wrong turning and wandered along this cliff path, part of which had been washed away in a downpour. There was a gap of about twenty feet in this rather steep hillside and a gang of workmen were trying to put it back together again. Meanwhile they had rigged up some ropes, so if you felt brave you could kind of abseil across – which in a rather foolhardy manner we did. It was a very cold day and I was muffled up in this vast blue anorak with the hood pulled tight around my face, leaving a gap no bigger than your hand through which I could see out. As we approached I heard one of the workmen say to his mate: 'Will you look, it's the bloke out of *'Allo 'Allo.'* I should add we were still thirty or forty yards away. I have no chance!

I am aware that I am about as typecast as you can get. There is really no point in worrying about it any more. Recently I helped an elderly lady across the road on a zebra crossing – she looked a little nervous and in need of assistance. We got halfway across when she stopped dead – with impatient motorists preparing to whizz by on either side – turned to me and said with some dismay: 'You are not French.'

'No,' I said. 'That's right, I'm not.'

'Oh dear, that has rather shattered my illusion,' she replied.

I had to tell her there was not a great deal I could do about that.

When there are children around I usually put on the René accent. It does happen that I go out to dinner with friends and the waiter might come and say: 'Excuse me, Mr Kaye, there's a little girl over there who would like your autograph. Can I bring her over?'

I say yes. And then when she comes over, of course, I 'ave to do it as René, do I not? I 'ave to say: ''allo, and 'ow are you?'

And when she replies I say: 'Oh, so you speak ze French, do you?'

She will say no, and so I say: 'But then 'ow do you understand what I am saying?'

Some children will go into a funny accent. But most of them are completely unphased and just chatter along in English.

Meanwhile I become aware of certain despairing groans and eyes to heaven from my friends. After all, when you think about it, here is this grown man, in his late forties, yapping away to a child in a bloody silly French accent.

I felt I couldn't help the lady on the pedestrian crossing but I do try not to destroy the illusion for children. I don't want them to come over to me and feel they have the wrong man – for it not to seem real any more. It's a bit like being Father Christmas. I find myself doing it to adults as well if there are kids around. It's sometimes a bit bizarre, and I feel obliged to apologise to the grown-ups afterwards.

Having said that, I use René for after-dinner speeches, presenting awards, all that sort of thing. Shy Gorden couldn't do these things at all. As René it is quite easy.

Yet when I was growing up I certainly did not seem to be cut out for any kind of showbusiness existence. I made my stage début at the Palace Theatre in Huddersfield at the age of eight or nine. And I was not a triumph.

It was a travelling show version of what was then a popular Sunday lunchtime radio programme called *Down in the Valley* with Big Bill Campbell and the Smith Brothers. This was partly a Wild West Show and partly a singalong with the Smith Brothers. I still remember them vividly. There were five of them and they would say, 'We are Mr and Mrs Smith's five little boys saying to you hallo, hallo, hallo, hallo, hallo.' Which remains two and a half times more hallos than I have to this day – but there you are.

So the show came to town and my parents took me along, and it was all great excitement. There was a bucking bronco race for children who were invited on stage. They had these little Muffin the Mule-type things on wheels which you sat on and rode. Now all the children who wanted to take part had to stand up, and they had some tin trays on stage with which they shone reflected light into the faces of the chosen ones. This light stopped just momentarily on me and I was sure from the beginning that the whole thing was a dreadful mistake. Certainly I was quite convinced it wasn't me they wanted. But my mum and dad pushed me.

So I sheepishly made my way down those stone steps from the upper circle and was hoisted aboard this blessed mule. I could just feel the organisers thinking this one shouldn't be here. He's too big. Well, they started the race, and my mule wouldn't move because I was so heavy. All the other kiddies went scuttling across the stage and I was marooned at the starting line. They had to ask me to alight, thank me for my trouble, and send me scurrying back up those steps again. I was totally mortified and practically in tears.

My shyness and feeling of awkwardness has been with me all

my life. I still hide behind humour, and occasionally I hide behind René. And I really do believe that René has a mind of his own. Now, after seven years of playing him, when I put on his apron and his waistcoat it is as if he takes me over.

René and I have come a long way together. I wonder sometimes what he would have made of Gorden Kaye, the ungainly Huddersfield schoolboy of forty years ago.

Chapter Two

Even the Birds Woke Up Coughing

I was a miracle baby. They tell me my first taste of fame came when I was far too young to appreciate it. I had just been born. My mother was forty-two years old. Both the *Daily Herald* and the *Daily Express* carried news stories about us. Giving birth for the first time at forty-two may be nothing to women now, but then it was a sensation – well, it was 1941.

My mother had suffered the familiar fate of many young women brought up in the Victorian and Edwardian era, albeit the end of it. She was the second youngest of a family of seven, and it somehow fell to her to stay at home looking after her parents. So when she finally married in 1939 she was already a good age – forty. I was her first and only child.

Indeed by the time I was fourteen or fifteen years old I had the impression that I was going to come home from school and my parents would be dead. I used to worry about it. They were so much older than my mates' parents. Their parents were in their early thirties and mine were in their fifties. Once I went into a local sweet shop with my mum and the lady took her to be my gran. I remember being very embarrassed by this, and it added to my feeling that my parents were going to pop their clogs at any moment.

It has to be said that as a child I was cossetted as much as the family income would allow – my father was an engineer in a tractor factory for most of the time.

I was a longed for child, and a rather unexpected one too.

It is no longer a secret that I am homosexual. And I suppose my early background does fit a little into that stereotype image of the gay man who has been over-protected by his parents. But I would not really like to blame them at all for the way I turned out to be. And in any case I don't really think that blame is the right word.

Both my parents loved me, of that I was always sure. And love can never do any kid much harm. But I suppose being somewhat over-protected – it was always don't go here, don't talk to strangers – and being given quite overpowering affection, particularly from my mother, made me very self-conscious. I was a plain kid, you see, and a bit podgy; quite a lot podgy, in fact. And I was painfully aware of how I looked, of my size, of my clumsiness, and of this dodgy left eye which pointed the wrong way all the time.

Anyway, when I first hit the headlines by being born, wartime Huddersfield was the foggiest place in Britain. We used to say we would wake up in the mornings to the sound of the birds coughing. My home town was a centre of the textile and chemical industries. When smokeless fuel came in later on it became as clear as anywhere else in Britain. But in those days it was like Los Angeles – the smog was always with you. The only time it was ever clear was during the 'Wakes Weeks' – two weeks' holiday in July and August when the whole town closed down and everybody went to Blackpool. I am as proud as any Yorkshireman of my birthplace and nobody is allowed to say a word against it except me – but in those days you couldn't even see it.

You could feel it, though, all around you. And I remember the heat. It is true, I am sure – not a trick of memory – that year after year we had scorching summers. Those were heady days, somehow. Whole families used to sit outside their front doors at night. The streets were baked in the sun all day, and it was just too hot to go to bed. People would squat on their scrubbed doorsteps in the pink evening glow and read the papers until darkness fell, and afterwards gossip late into the night. The smells were of bacon frying and potato soup, pipe smoke and onions and milk boiling over, forgotten on somebody's stove. The sounds were of babies crying and dogs barking and children playing, wirelesses whistling unheeded on hidden kitchen tables. The background noises of other people's lives, their chatter, their laughter, and sometimes their quarrels. We children used to wander around the streets half naked in little flip-flops or bare feet – not because our families were too poor to afford proper shoes, but simply because it was so warm.

I had an extremely happy, cared for childhood. It wasn't easy being brought up during the war by very working-class parents. Though I wouldn't say it was exactly tough, either. But there wasn't a lot of money flying about, and I suppose that has somehow inspired me throughout my life to get up and get out of it. I believed there was something better out there!

A lot of my Socialist friends still up North see me as a turncoat and reckon that I have become very middle-class. I think I have got it about right, because while my Socialist friends call me a Fascist, my Conservative friends call me a Commie.

As a kid all I knew was that you just got on with the job of surviving. My parents may have spoiled me, but I had to behave myself. I had to go to bed when I was told and eat up my greens. The money limited the material side of things. It was simple food, simple toys – and simple behaviour too.

I wouldn't say I was a strange child, but awkward is a good word to describe me. I was very shy, dreadfully introverted. I would blush easily. If I was asked by the bus conductor: 'Have you nothing smaller?', I would practically burst into tears.

My mother had a sister called Bessie who used to come by rail from Glasgow to visit us, and I was sent to meet her at Leeds Station to help her change from the big express to the small Huddersfield puffer. Aunt Bessie was a wonderful lady, a spinster of the true Presbyterian type and very imposing in her stark black, with neat hat firmly pinned dead straight on the top of her head. She was always causing me great embarrassment as a boy. I was permanently crimson when Aunt Bessie was around.

To start with, she would arrive for two weeks with steamer trunks looking as if she was planning to stay six months. She would imperiously summon some poor little Yorkshire porter whom she would browbeat into lugging these great things right across Leeds Station to the Huddersfield platform, which was as far away as you could get. When they had loaded the last of these huge pieces of baggage on to the local train the porters, somewhat understandably, used to stand around with their hands held out expectantly. Aunt Bessie would cross their palms with half a dozen Smarties. I couldn't look.

We would then board the train home, and if it was full Aunt Bessie would order in a tone of voice that demanded immediate obedience: 'Arms up.' Everyone would meekly raise their seat arm-rests and shift closer together, thus creating more room in the carriage. Aunt Bessie and I would squeeze into the resulting gaps and we would all travel to Huddersfield in total discomfort.

I remember her once taking me out for tea in Huddersfield to one of those rather elegant little cafés with linen tablecloths and silver teapots and china teacups and a musical trio playing discreetly in the corner – the sort of place that was a part of the culture of Northern towns then but no longer exists today. Going out with Aunt Bessie was always a liability for poor shy me, and on this occasion she excelled herself. She discovered a hairline crack in her teacup, promptly snapped her fingers for the waitress and demanded to see the manager.

'There is a crack in this cup. It is unhygienic and a hazard to health and you must break it at once,' she instructed him.

Being a sensible fellow the manager recognized immediately that he had met more than his match. He agreed readily and was about to take the offending article away – but that was not good enough for my Aunt Bessie.

'You will break it here at the table, young man, if you please,' she told him.

And so he had to fetch a towel and wrap this cup up and break it in front of her, while Aunt Bessie nodded her head approvingly. Well, everyone in the place was rubbernecking in our direction and I was the colour of freshly boiled beetroot. I think my whole body was blushing. I could not believe that even she could go this far.

Being terribly introverted stayed with me until I was grown up. Not only did I feel that the whole world was conspiring to embarrass me, but I also reckoned that I was always making a prat of myself. I remember as a seven or eight-year-old I had this little bathing costume – an original one-piece over-the-shoulder job. It was yellow with brown stripes. We used to go and play in some local playing fields and I would wear this bathing costume. I must have been quite a sight – a podgy, slightly discoloured wasp on two legs.

One day I had been off playing, and on my way home I was standing outside the radio shop just staring in the window. Radio shops were very exciting to us in those days. The only thing was I had this bathing suit slung over my shoulder by the strap for some reason, and I was standing there in the nuddy. A neighbour came along and saw me and persuaded me to put it back on. I did so, and I got my head through the leg hole and one arm through the other leg hole, and my legs through the arm straps so the bits that should have been covered were actually not covered at all. Dangling, in fact.

I arrived home in that state. Sometimes when I look back at that sort of thing and at photographs of me as a child, I still cringe. I don't have any photographs of that incident, I'm glad to say, but things like that seemed to be a daily event.

As I grew older I became all too aware of my awkwardness, and the self-consciousness increased with the years, reaching its peak in my teens and early twenties. I suppose since then I have capitalized on it. I know people will sometimes laugh at me when I just scratch my ear or shake my head or something, and all of that has become part of my trade.

When you are growing up, though, it's not so easy. I never seemed to be able to get anything quite right. I had been left at home once when I was probably nine or ten while my mother went shopping. It was a terrible winter's day, snow everywhere, a blizzard blowing. We lived in a Victorian terraced house and the main water pipe ran up beside the front door, and was not very well protected. Suddenly the pipe burst and water was gushing all over the front hallway.

So I put on my brand-new shiny wellingtons and my little coat and ran off down the road to the greengrocer's – not very far, two or three hundred yards down the road. But being brand-new wellingtons they were tied together with a bit of string. And being a prat from an early age, I did nothing about this. By the time I got to the greengrocer's I was wet through because I had fallen down so many times in the slush. They gazed at me in amazement and then they just said, 'Come on lad, come here', and they cut me free with a pair of scissors.

They remembered that for many years, because, like in a lot of provincial places, the greengrocer's had been there for ever and never changed. The people who worked there just got older. There was not the changeover of staff there is in shops now. So as a young man in long trousers, twenty years old or whatever, they would always make some crack about my wellies.

I was invariably trying so hard and getting things ever so slightly, but quite disastrously, wrong. That's what I mean about being awkward.

My gran used to live with us. She was bedridden and she had a bed in the front room. One day when my mum had gone shopping, poor granny wanted the bedpan. That was when I was about seven or eight and already trying badly to be grown-up and capable. So I set about the task required. And I managed to get it organized, too, except that I put her on back to front. We will not go into the results.

On another occasion, I remember, my father, who was always a great gardener – he was so good all the neighbours used to bring us their poorly plants and he would nurse them back to health – had put in six tomato plants. When he came home from work that day he had twelve plants because I'd cut the top of each of the nice little green shoots and replanted them. They all died, of course.

They were good days, though, they really were. We had a lot of fun at home. The family were all great card players and we used to play for halfpennies. Aunt Bessie was a bit of a star again because being strict Presbyterian she could not play for money, not even halfpennies, so she would use matchsticks. The only thing was that when she won, everybody else's halfpennies went straight into her handbag. Her religion also prevented her from drinking alcohol, allegedly, but I remember one sterling New Year's Eve when her neat tonic water was being gently laced with gin, which she pretended not to notice. And I am sure it must have been a pretence. She became drunker and drunker and more and more outrageous and started dancing and kicking her legs in the air. The next morning not a word was said.

My mother's sisters figured greatly in my childhood. My Auntie Marjorie, the youngest, was the one who looked after everyone and kept us all together until her death in 1987 at the age of eighty-six. She was a great character. I remember once going to Majorca on holiday when it was very hot. I came home and told Auntie Marjorie that it had been 80 degrees in the shade. 'Oh,' she said. 'I don't think I could have stayed in the shade then, it would be too hot for me.' She was the family chronicler and the leading light of my *This Is Your Life* show, and there will be more of her later.

Then there was Auntie May who married a farmer called Walter and they lived up in the Dales at Ingleton near the Lancashire–Yorkshire border. I used to spend holidays on their farm and I loved every minute of it – like all townies, I am a countryman at heart. Recently I went back there and drove through this little place called Coldcotes – only a collection of houses really – just outside of Ingleton, and I noticed a gatepost which is still on the skew where I hit it with the tractor thirty-three years ago as a boy of fifteen. I also came across this flat space by the roadside where there used to be a henhouse where I would collect the eggs.

The memories came flooding back. I have travelled the world and been to some incredible places, but I think a yearning for your roots remains with you always. When I get out of bed early in the morning and drive up the M1 and I know I will soon be in my beloved Yorkshire, I feel a real thrill. That day in Coldcotes I could clearly see inside my head a picture of the old roadside henhouse all those years ago and me plodding up the lane in my wellies clutching a bucket. I would take corn to feed the chickens and then I would put the eggs in the bucket, and I invariably took home the pot egg which Uncle Walter put under the hens to make them lay, and I would have to go all the way back with it. It was quite a step from the farm to that henhouse, and I think the family used to send me there to get me out from under their feet.

My older cousin and I would pick mushrooms early in the

morning and set up a stall on the Skipton–Lancaster main road to sell our freshly gathered harvest to passing motorists. I could never get over how quickly mushrooms grew. We would pull them out of the ground one day and the next they would be back again in the same place.

On Uncle Walter's land I learned to hunt rabbits with a ferret and to milk a cow by hand. I wasn't ever very sure about rabbiting, but I did it, and I could get a cow to yield milk all right, even if with not much efficiency.

I loved that farm, but apparently when I was a toddler of two or three I nearly came a real cropper. I went missing and they found me in a pen with Uncle Walter's ferocious bull. I was right underneath the beast, examining its nether regions. The family were petrified and Uncle Walter very slowly and very quietly came over and lifted me, blissfully unaware of any danger, to safety.

Huddersfield was a grim industrial town, but you could be up in those hills among the green fields and the trees, bowed and twisted by the weather, and the wild, wind-scoured moorland in ten minutes. It was not a bad place at all to grow up.

Even the war didn't seem so dreadful to me as a child. I was only four when it ended, so I knew nothing else and I remember no sense of fear. But I do quite clearly remember the doodlebugs coming over and my parents telling me to run downstairs to the air-raid shelters. The stairs would be shaking and my dad would be at the bottom of the stairs holding me and my mother would be at the top and the whole staircase would be moving beneath us. The Germans were looking for the local ICI factory, which they used to bomb regularly.

My father was a wagon driver during the war, and for quite a time afterwards. He was too old for the army, but he was in the ARP. He did the *Dad's Army* night watchman bit during the blackouts – put those lights out and all of that. And he would drive ammunition about.

I always had a terrific sense of security at home. But there were certain things that scared me as a child which have stayed with me to this day.

Our Victorian terraced house basically consisted of two rooms downstairs and two bedrooms upstairs – only there was a big attic at the top and a huge cellar down below. It had been a storage cellar and there was a great stone table in the middle of it. There was also an incredible stone boiler with a fire blazing beneath it in which, in those long-ago days before washing machines, we used to boil our clothes. Down a step was a partitioned area that was the coal cellar. I used to have nightmares that I heard a noise and I had to go down to that coal cellar in the dark and something evil was lurking there – I was never sure what, or why I thought it. But I know I still get that strange dream when I am back in Huddersfield – I still wake up in a cold sweat convinced there is something horrid in the cellar, and I still dislike places like that.

Then there was my brush with a swarm of daddy long legs. I was about eight or nine and we had been blackberrying up in the hills and were walking along a narrow, stinging nettle-lined path between two fields. We had not noticed that this little lane, with a wall on either side, was full of daddy long legs at ground level. And as we progressed along the path they flew up like a cloud of locusts and they were in our hair, in our eyes, and in our mouths. We had no choice but to keep walking forward through this fog of flying insects. I have never forgotten it, and if there is a daddy long legs around I am afraid it has to die before I can settle. They say the creatures only live for twenty-four hours, but they do not live for twenty-four seconds when I am around. I can still feel them pressed all around my face.

I think my dreadful self-consciousness was partly due to my dodgy eye, in which as a small child I was almost totally blind. People still notice this left eye, which goes in and out when I am tired or when I am poorly or whatever. But when I was a kid it was much worse – it pointed in completely the wrong direction all the time.

It all began when I was three and we were having a Christmas party. My mother smoked. She didn't smoke much longer after this incident, but she smoked then. I was sitting on her knee and she had a cigarette going. I got hold of her cig and I had a puff of it. It made me cough and choke and cry and I became quite hysterical. I scratched her face and I fell on to the floor in a very violent trauma and rolled under the table. Apparently when they settled me down my left eye had gone right into the corner. There had been some kind of tension there, and maybe this sort of fit I had caused a weak muscle in it to collapse.

One thing is certain – I quite clearly do remember this incident even though I was so young. Many of these childhood stories I was actually told about by my parents when I was older – but this I vividly remember. I can still feel it happening.

It was quite serious. The sight went to a great extent, leaving me with just 20 per cent vision in that eye. I wore glasses with a patch over one side for years to try and strengthen the weak eye. Then when I was eleven I was operated on in Huddersfield Royal Infirmary by a Mr Gamm, a strange name I shall always remember.

They gave me a pre-med injection that was supposed to knock me out. Then they came back an hour later with the trolley, having had the lunch break in between, I think. They had left me longer than they should have done and I just hopped out of bed and hopped on the trolley when I was supposed to be zonked. I clearly wasn't, so they had to give me another dose.

But the clearest memory of all is being blind for two weeks when both my eyes were covered with pads because I couldn't bear the light. As I couldn't see to feed myself, everything was fed to me. Liquids, like weak tea and orange juice, came through a spout from a feeder. Everything else was fed to me in sandwich form. That was OK. The ham sandwiches and the chicken paste sandwiches were fine. But the fried tomato sandwiches were a revelation. They were certainly not toasted or anything sophisticated like that. Just soggy white bread with this goo inside – which, strangely enough, wasn't all that unpalatable. But the mess that I was more or less permanently covered in from this gunk, apparently had to be seen to be believed. And I couldn't see at all, of course.

It was a nice feeling, though, when the pads came off eventually and I could see so much better and the left eye was straighter than ever before. I used to wander around and talk to all the old guys in the hospital. I think it may have been because of that experience that, when I was older and needed something to fill my spare time and force me to become more extrovert, hospital broadcasting appealed to me. And it was hospital broadcasting which would set me on the path that eventually led to wonderful *'Allo 'Allo* and the character it seemed I had been waiting all my life to become – René Artois.

Chapter Three

The René I Know

In 1987 I was invited to address the Water Rats at the Grosvenor House Hotel. They are a charitable body of some of the finest entertainers in the world, including a very large selection of top comics, and I was supposed to be there to make them laugh.

The King Rat at the time was Danny La Rue, and other guests included Mr and Mrs Jimmy Tarbuck, Mr and Mrs Des O'Connor, Mr and Mrs Barry Humphries, Mr and Mrs Bob Monkhouse, Mr and Mrs Elton John, Mr and Mrs Charlton Heston and Mr and Mrs Michael Parkinson. The top table upon which, as guest speaker, I was seated, was raised from the body of the hall and it felt a bit like a re-enactment of the Last Supper. I was scared to death.

But thankfully my good friend René was very cool about the whole thing and did just fine. 'As a café owner myself I know just what difficulty there is in providing food for all this lot. Of course in my case my customers do not know which knives and forks to use, either,' said René.

David Croft believes that I become taken over by René when I am working on 'Allo 'Allo, the reaction that happens to most actors, and he says: 'During rehearsals and filming they actually become the characters they are playing. When they take a different part they move on to that. My daughter Penny is married to Simon Cadell, who was such a success in *Hi-De-Hi!* He is inclined to play bad guys a lot, so for much of the time when he is working she

24

keeps out of his way, because he is apt to carry on being them at home.'

The take-over theory is one I go along with to some extent. Although I am not quite sure what I make of David Croft's potted history of René and Edith.

'René was born a year or two or three or four before the turn of the century in Nancy. The Artois were a small family mostly of boys and girls, the male side being known as the Nancy Boys.

'He has been married to Edith for twenty-one years. He is a firm devotee of pre- and post-marital sex – as long as it is not with the wife.

'René is a reluctant, local, unpaid, acting member of the Resistance and a part-time collaborator. At the end of hostilities he may well be in line for head-shaving, but, taking into account the rate at which his hair is tumbling on to the bedroom carpet, nature may well deprive the vengeful mob of that pleasure.

'René's wife Edith was born before the turn of the century on a date which has been smudged from her birth certificate. Suffice it to say that the document is distinctly yellowed at the edges, so it can be assumed that Edith is well past her "best before" date.

'Edith married René in a moment of pique when she discovered him looking through the keyhole of her bedroom door. René thought it was the bedroom door of one of the waitresses, but he could hardly advance that as an excuse.'

Whatever his past, René is wonderful to hide behind and the jokes seem to come easily when he is on his feet.

I had taken Carmen Silvera, René's wife Edith, to the dinner as my guest and I was able to say: 'I see that my wife is seated this evening next to Mr Des O'Connor. Perhaps 'e can give 'er a few tips on singing.' That was good for a few laughs, and the biggest one of all came from Des himself who is all too aware of the many gags about his voice.

Then I addressed King Rat himself, Danny La Rue. 'I first met Mr La Rue during the early days of the war,' I related. 'He has not changed a bit. He looks exactly the same now as 'e did then. Rumour 'as it that 'e has a picture of Dolores Gray in his attic.'

This was actually my first attempt at after-dinner speaking of this kind. Not only did it lead to my eventually becoming a Water Rat myself, of which I am very proud, but also to a regular round of speechmaking.

I have on several occasions made speeches at functions hosted by Prince Edward, who I am delighted to say is a big *'Allo 'Allo* fan. On 14 March 1989 he brought four hundred people to the stage show and afterwards they all went on to a charity dinner at the London Hilton Hotel. Carmen and I and some of the other members of cast were invited to join them – she sat on the Prince's left, and I was opposite him. A couple of trumpeters trumpeted the guests into the room. It was quite a formal occasion, lightened by the Prince who proved himself to be an accomplished joke-teller. He told one joke which was, as befitted the occasion, French. Although I am sworn to secrecy as to its content, should His Royal Highness ever wish to give up being a prince and take up the role of stand-up comic, he could earn a decent living.

I write my own speeches as René, and try to come up with lines which are appropriate for the event. Hopefully it looks spontaneous on the night, but in fact I research quite thoroughly for a couple of weeks before. If it is going to work for me I have to know my subject, and the audience must also be familiar with my subject.

Once I was asked to make a speech for Richard Branson. I said: 'I understand that Richard Branson runs an airline called Virgin. Why anyone wants to fly with an airline that is not prepared to go all the way I cannot understand.' Getting things slightly wrong is a René trademark. I went on to confuse condoms with compact discs. 'Mr Branson manufactures condoms,' I said. 'I understand he even has one of these CD factories in the middle of Oxford Street.'

I also played a part in the Variety Club's tribute to Bill Cotton the year he retired as managing director of the BBC. I would not say I made a speech. It was more a question of interrupting Bill's speech – as arranged, of course.

Dressed as René – naturally – I blundered noisily up to the top table just as Bill was getting into full flight, reading detailed extracts from his thirty-year diary at the BBC. I elbowed him out of the way and started noisily rearranging the table. When he protested

I told him to take no notice of me. 'I'm sorry, we 'ave to clear up,' I said. 'Tonight we 'ave an important function.'

I went on to pinch a look at his list of BBC people to thank and to tell him why he should not bother with most of them. 'We can lose him for a start – I've just seen him in the bar, and he's blitzed out of his head,' I said. 'That one has gone to Channel Four. . . . Look here, Mr Cotton, half of these people you never liked, and the other half never liked you.'

The assembled diners, many of them those in question from the BBC, fell about. René can get away with murder. I would never dare say such things as Gorden.

At that original Water Rats dinner Jimmy Tarbuck said that one of the reasons for my success, certainly at a gathering like that, is that I am not a stand-up comic and so none of the others see me as a threat. They can all laugh at me without worrying that maybe I'm telling the gags better than they do.

At the time of writing I have made ten appearances on Terry Wogan's *Wogan* programme, and for one of these I re-wrote the lyrics of 'Chorus Line' which was then sung by the entire *'Allo 'Allo* cast. The René/Gorden version was directed at Terry along these lines:

> You were tops on Radio Two, Tel;
> Now it's down to auto-cue, Tel.

I don't think Marvin Hamlisch has much to worry about – we got his permission, incidentally, before tampering with his song – but we all had a lot of fun.

I think probably René's most successful personal appearance of all was at Christchurch Races in New Zealand during the tour of the *'Allo 'Allo* stage show there in the autumn of 1988. One of the radio/TV stations there asked me to go along and do a little piece before the major race – it was like a big Derby-style afternoon. I did it all as René off duty, wearing a straw hat, and discussed what I was going to back.

Incredibly enough, I had never been to a race meeting in my life before. And providentially, in view of the show's long-running

'Madonna with ze big boobies' joke, there was a horse running called Miss Madonna – which gave me my jokes for the afternoon. 'It is bound to be well out in front,' I said. And to put my money where my mouth was I placed a bet of 25 dollars each way, which was all I had in my pocket, on this creature about which I knew very little except I was told the odds were rather long.

After doing my bit on TV I was taken up to the Jockey Club box where everyone was drinking their gin and tonics and scotch, and I had my ginger ale because I don't like alcohol, and we walked out on to the balcony to watch the race. I was given the biggest pair of binoculars you have ever seen and the sun was shining and there was a lot of cheering, and I thought, this is exciting. Then Miss Madonna came around the corner in second place, steaming down the home straight 200 yards from the winning post, straining for victory. By then I thought it was all absolutely thrilling. And my horse won by a nose. I couldn't believe it. I picked up 586 dollars, and Richard Marner, Colonel Von Strohm, was there, tickled to bits at my reaction. He actually lives in Newmarket, and his world revolves around horses.

When I had calmed down a little the TV cameras returned and there I was counting the money. There was some magic involved there somewhere. Nothing like it would ever happen to Gorden Kaye. René was just able to say: 'It is very easy zis 'orse racing. You just put ze money on and zen you win.'

The longest laugh I was ever involved in as René happened when we were recording an episode of the TV series and it lasted for thirty-seven seconds. Maria, the waitress, had left the Café René, having escaped from a prisoner-of-war camp. She had disguised herself as a parcel, but had not used enough stamps, and was sent back to the Red Cross in Geneva. So René was looking for a new waitress and one of the girls he interviewed was – in real life too, actually – an acrobat. She launched herself into this rather suggestive crablike position and just held it. It was all rather rude and René was having the vapours, and the audience started to laugh and would not stop. I had the next line, which I could not deliver because of the prolonged laughter. When I did manage to speak the audience over-reacted with a round of applause. The director could not sustain one shot for that long and so kept cutting away to the other characters – he had to have somewhere to put his scissors, somewhere to edit the film. It upset me greatly that the BBC cut it before the show was transmitted, because I reckon it must have been one of the longest laughs in the history of sitcom.

I still remember the sweet sound of that audience laughter in my ears the first time I ever played René in the pilot of *'Allo 'Allo*. I was behind the bar wearing the René apron and waistcoat for the first time and had been told by the Resistance that Monsieur LeClerc, the forger originally played by Jack Haig – who sadly died in July 1989 – would come into the café in disguise and ask for a cognac. Now we were supposed to speak in code. He should then have taken out a cigar and asked me for a light and I should have replied that I had no matches.

Instead this other character came into the café and ordered a cognac. I asked him if he would like a light. He replied, 'Thank you.' I said I didn't have any matches and he then asked me why I had offered him a light.

By this time the whole thing has started to fall apart in true *'Allo 'Allo* style and I ask him if he is one of them. My customer begins to cheer up noticeably and starts to tell me how lonely he has been on the Russian front. Then you realize that not only is this character gay, which is what he meant by agreeing that he was one of them, but he is also a Nazi, Lieutenant Gruber. René starts to panic and get into a complete flap with himself – and the audience were laughing so hard the studio microphones had to be turned down.

It was quite a moment. All our worries disappeared. We had fretted that maybe the audience would not grasp when the two British airmen arrived, that all the rest of us were not supposed to understand them because they, of course, were speaking English, and what we were speaking was French. But we need not have worried. The audience picked up on it straightaway. And they quickly cottoned on, when our two airmen could not work out why every passing motorist was hooting at them, that it was because they were riding their bicycles on the wrong side of the road.

René is quite reliable in a way, I think, which is something people seem to like about him. His job is to react to all the other people in the show, and he does so often with only a look. Michelle from the Resistance will come up with her catchphrase: 'Listen very carefully, I will say this only once,' and René just rolls his eyes resignedly skywards. In one scene in the stage show I am in bed with Edith and she turns to me and says very seriously: 'René, if there is anyone else, I will kill myself.' I just look at her – for ever. Finally I say: 'How?' The audience adore it.

You see, he has that little surprise line at the end, but in general you know how René is going to react to most situations and also just how far he will go. *'Allo 'Allo* is quite naughty and suggestive – particularly the stage version – but you know exactly where it will stop.

Also in the stage show there is a scene when Gruber, the gay lieutenant, comes into the café to find René bent over the back of an inflatable dummy. Now the audience know very well it is an inflatable dummy and know exactly what is going on, but they laugh at Gruber seeing what he thinks he sees. It is the same thing with the pop-up sausage under René's apron. René has a sausage under his apron, which he could actually carry out in the open but that would ruin the joke, and sooner or later you know he is going to sit down and that the sausage will pop up beneath the apron, and Lieutenant Gruber will think it is something else.

It is all wonderfully predictable, and it's bawdy. It's ooh-la-la in fact. It is not for prudish people, but for general middle-of-the-road-folk and I think it is fairly inoffensive. And because of that predictability and familiarity with the characters, particularly René, it is safe. You know very well that René will never get his hands down Yvette's blouse. He will nearly do so, but will always be thwarted at the last minute. The audience trusts us on *'Allo 'Allo* not to go over the edge – and we never do.

I think another of René's strengths is that the audience does maintain sympathy with him even though he is so dreadful. He is a lovable rogue, with the Germans breathing down his neck in one direction, Edith coming at him from another and stopping his bit of how's-your-father with the waitresses, and Michelle from the

Resistance pushing him to do his duty because if he doesn't he will be shot as a collaborator.

We do not use René's accent for laughs in itself. He was never supposed to be a Clouseau character. If you think about it, Inspector Clouseau got laughs on his accent because he was a Frenchman speaking English. I am not. I am a Frenchman speaking French and I can get nothing out of funny pronunciations.

But mistakes in pronunciation do make me laugh a lot personally. I was on a touring holiday in France once with a friend and we were having a drink in our hotel bar when a British colonel type came up to us and invited us to join him and his wife simply on the basis that we were the only other English people there. We did so, and he asked us if we were heading home. We said that indeed we were on our way to catch the ferry at Calais. He replied: 'Oh, the wife and I always go from Bolone.' And he pronounced Boulogne just like that in his terribly public school accent – Bolone. His wife said it exactly the same way, and my friend and I enjoyed ourselves thoroughly, spending the rest of the evening baiting them both into repeating 'Bolone' as many times as possible.

Beryl Reid, who is a pal of mine, once had a dresser who talked about going on holiday to Torrymollynos and Malarga rather than Torremolinos or Malaga. And all these lovely mispronunciations have gone into my personal humorous vocabulary.

But my René accent is very slight, which does make it easy for me to drop into. It is also very familiar. It is a bit like Yorkshire – you just drop the aitches. 'Oh 'eck' sounds much the same in a Yorkshire accent as in a French accent, so I can improvise quite quickly. David Croft's co-writer Jeremy Lloyd is inclined to capitalize on this, and if he has a last-minute idea, thinks nothing of slipping me another half-dozen lines or so just before the recording. Jeremy is brilliant at grabbing you by the lapels even while you are filming and changing just two words, which then have the audience in fits.

I do get a laugh, though, once again not out of the accent itself, but out of inverting words or phrases in the way the French do. They don't have any apostrophes, and the slightly stilted style of speech which we use gives us a special flavour. I say: 'But for the sake of 'eaven, what are you doing?'. Not 'For heaven's sake.'

The fact that I can slip into this accent so easily off screen means I can use René as a front whenever it suits me. Certainly I much prefer him to take over on public occasions – he makes much better speeches than I do.

Chapter Four

The Making of 'Allo 'Allo

Little Mimi, sporting a moustache, a top hat, a frock coat and baggy black trousers, was staggering beneath the weight of a coffin. She was landed with the heavy end, naturally. At the front was tall, gangly Crabtree, Arthur Bostrom, whose only carrying problem had come earlier when he announced: 'The hindle has come off the coffin.' Trotting along behind were Monsieur Alfonse, the undertaker, and Monsieur LeClerc, the burglar and getaway driver. They paused only to stage a sword fight over a matter of honour.

René had enough problems already, dealing with a wife wearing not only the trousers but also a red beard. With a great many of his exasperated long-suffering looks he struggled to part the pair of ageing duellists while looking over his shoulder for any signs of lurking Germans.

After all, the famous café owner, his wife, his waitresses and all the other gallant freedom fighters were actually inside Nazi HQ in the heart of occupied France. Dressed as undertakers, they were trying to rescue the two British airmen – who never seem quite able to escape – by spiriting them away inside a pair of coffins.

'It should flippin' well look realistic,' said four-foot-ten Sue Hodge, who appeared on the point of collapse beneath her coffin load. 'I can barely lift the thing.'

'Allo 'Allo's senior citizens, actors Kenneth Connor and Derek Royle as Alfonse and LeClerc, were also a little the worse for wear, having spent two days filming a very active scene in some of the highest temperatures of a much hotter than usual British summer. The entire cast, including the women, were dressed for the sequence in undertakers' toppers and frock coats. Carmen Silvera as Edith was suffering from the sudden growth of her rather itchy beard. 'It is driving me quite mad,' she told me, 'particularly in this heat.' Resistance girl Michelle, played by Kirsten Cooke, was as relentlessly dedicated as usual in the coffin-carrying line-up along with Yvette, played by Vicki Michelle. Both of them and Sue Hodge as Mimi had 'grown' moustaches.

Chaos and calamity threatened from all directions. *'Allo 'Allo* was on location again for its latest series – and the situation was absolutely as normal.

Command HQ is in fact rambling Lynford Hall, a few miles out of Swaffham in Norfolk. The countryside around there is very like parts of France. It has the added advantage that it is just a couple of hours from London and everybody speaks English. Therefore it works out much cheaper than going to France – we can probably shoot for three weeks on location in Norfolk for the price of just one week in France. And we all know that the choice of location has absolutely nothing to do with the fact that David Croft lives in the area.

Lynford Hall itself took five years to build between 1857 and 1862. It was commissioned by a man called Lyne Stephens who inherited a fortune from his glass manufacturer father. Lyne Stephens had the house constructed after the style of a French château for his Parisienne ballet dancer wife, Yolande Marie Louise Duvernay. He died before the house was completed, but his widow lived there until her death more than thirty years later.

Because of its French architecture Lynford Hall – now a motel and conference centre – lends itself admirably to the purposes of *'Allo 'Allo* and has become the show's most popular location base. With the help of a selection of swastikas and Nazi eagles, a few portraits of Hitler, the odd construction of elaborate polystyrene plaster work and the occasional false BBC wall, the Hall makes a perfect German HQ. One of its courtyards, lined with false shop fronts, has been used in earlier episodes as *'Allo 'Allo*'s village square.

A TV show on location calls for a great deal of rigmarole. The BBC sends a regular team of sixty crew and cast up to Norfolk during filming, taking over the pubs and restaurants around this quiet part of the country. The wedding scene shown in the latest series called for forty-two extras – so that day there were a total of 150 people, including additional make-up and costume men and women, on the set. The wardrobe department takes over a suite of rooms at the George Hotel, Swaffham, traditional home for most of the cast.

The *'Allo 'Allo* team, actors and crew, have been together a long time now. There have been few changes of cast since the 1982 pilot programme, and most of the crew have worked on the show since the beginning. So any kind of accident on set shakes everybody up. Early one morning during filming in June, an electrician fell dramatically from a rooftop and was rushed to hospital by ambulance. Several of the cast, including Carmen Silvera, saw him fall. It was an awful moment. He was lying on the ground moaning and we were all really afraid he had been seriously injured. Later everybody learned that was not the case. The man was just badly bruised – and had been allowed to go home. But cast and crew alike were shocked and upset and the accident had an unsettling effect on the morning's filming.

David Croft has a reputation for putting together happy TV shows – and *'Allo 'Allo* is no exception. When the good news about the electrician came through about lunchtime, everybody on set began noticeably to cheer up.

It is well known that armies march on their stomachs. Anybody who has ever visited a film set knows that, while talented writing, directing and acting may have a part to play, if the food is no good the entire production will collapse. During meal breaks, cast and crew descend upon vast quantities of supplies like a load of vultures. And sometimes it seems that the most important people on location are the caterers – in this case the three brothers Jeaffreson from Brighton, who relentlessly provide several gourmet meals a day from the seemingly impossible limitations of a kitchen in a caravan.

Lunch is always accompanied by plenty of banter between the cast and a selection of cringe-making pro gags. 'I can't stand your wife . . . well, leave her on the side of your plate then.' Off-camera jokes, however well tried and excruciatingly corny, help pass the time.

Filming can be a surprisingly tedious business. I am on screen for most of every show, yet I still spend much of my day waiting around. Props and lights have to be moved. Scenes painstakingly set up, rehearsed, then shot usually two or three times – and on the occasions when it all goes wrong, sometimes many more.

In fact, however, the latest series of eight *'Allo 'Allo* shows was filmed on location at a particularly fast rate. It had originally been planned to produce six shows. Eventually eight were decided upon, but the two and a half weeks arranged on location were not extended. So there was little room for mistakes up in Norfolk – and in addition to making everyone worry, that electrician's fall caused delays which further stretched the team.

As ever, we got through somehow. And during the summer we recorded every week on Friday nights at the BBC TV Centre. An audience watches the show performed live in the studio – with the location film inserted. At each recording I'm called upon to introduce my fellow cast members, and each week I strive to come up with something remotely amusing. A typical example would go along these lines: Helga (Kim Hartman): 'And now the young lady who makes the officers salute and the privates stand to attention.'

Of Mimi le Bonque (all four foot ten of Sue Hodge): 'An actress who can keep her ear to the ground without bending over.'

Of Yvette (Vicki Michelle): 'Last night she had an accident. She swerved to avoid a child and fell off the bed.'

Of Crabtree (Arthur Bostrom): 'A man who speaks the French language like a native – of Tanganyika.'

Of Edith's mother, Fanny (Fifi) Lafanne (Rose Hill): 'Tonight we have a cast of over seventy – and here she is.'

And of Edith herself (Carmen Silvera): 'Her singing voice was trained – then it escaped and returned to the wild.'

All the laughter you hear on the television programme is quite genuine. In this country, unlike America, canned laughter is frowned upon. Certainly a comedy producer of David Croft's calibre would not hear of it. The studio audience reaction is an important ingredient. Personally I need to hear that audience laugh. It brings it all alive for me. I know the *Yes Prime Minister* team once said they would prefer to record without an audience because they found the applause disturbing. But I like to feel there are people out there responding. I think all the cast does.

'Allo 'Allo has now been sold to more than thirty countries including France, and pulls in 16 million viewers here at home – coming top of the ratings behind only the blockbuster soaps *Coronation Street* and *EastEnders*. I know David Croft confidently expects that it is only a matter of time before it is sold to Germany. 'I am quite sure it will go there eventually,' he has told me with a chuckle. 'The Germans may not be thought to be terribly good at laughing at themselves – but neither are the French, and they seem to love it.'

'Allo 'Allo has become so well established and highly popular it is almost difficult to remember the flak it received in the early days. The programme came under heavy attack from those who felt strongly that the show's subject should never have been made into a laughing matter. Paul Fox, head of Yorkshire TV, may well be a little embarrassed to recall an impassioned speech he gave at the Edinburgh TV Festival, demanding to know what the BBC had come to making fun of wartime resistance in France. 'Do they really think this is funny?' he asked. Mr Fox is now Managing Director of the BBC – and if he still has personal doubts about one of the Corporation's most popular assets, he keeps quiet on the subject.

David Croft clearly finds the situation amusing, but also knows when it is politic to remain silent. He just says: 'Paul Fox is far too old a hand to let that early outburst cloud his judgement today.'

Newspaper critics, led by Herbert Kretzmer of the *Daily Mail*, expressed horror at the subject matter of *'Allo 'Allo*. Herbie was at the time one of the most respected of TV reviewers and is the lyricist for a blockbuster hit musical which itself takes an unlikely subject – *Les Misérables*, based on Victor Hugo's book about the French Revolution. He wrote:

The programme depicts the German military occupiers as kindly, harmless buffoons you wouldn't mind taking home to tea. They are jolly chaps who would never kill a mosquito unless they had to. It has been argued that the deliberate insensitivities of *'Allo 'Allo* are acceptable because the series does not pretend to be anything except a cheerful, knockabout farce, and that its French (sex-mad) and British (prize twits) characters are treated not much better. It is not a persuasive case. The French and British in wartime Europe did not cover the Continent with terror, or send millions of hand-picked civilians to agonizing death.

I must admit that while I never found the show's theme in any way offensive myself, I was not surprised by the level of reaction in the beginning. And I did, in fact, worry a little about the reaction of those who had lived through the occupation of France. I was greatly reassured about four years ago when I received a letter and a very special gift from a lady fan.

She was the widow of a Frenchman who had fought with the Resistance during the war. Her name was Mrs Benn, and her husband had watched two series of *'Allo 'Allo* before he died. She said in her letter that her husband had thoroughly enjoyed the programme, which he thought was hugely funny, and she enclosed his Free French badge, which was of considerable sentimental value, for me to keep and to wear. I am very proud of that and also felt that it indicated the right sort of feeling from the right quarter.

David and co-writer Jeremy Lloyd had no doubts about the programme from the moment they dreamed it up – and are quick to point out that it was never the intention of *'Allo 'Allo* to make fun of the French Resistance.

David Croft puts it this way: 'The aim was always to send up those heavy wartime drama series we seem to get so many of.' In fact it quickly became known that *Secret Army*, set in Belgium and starring Bernard Hepton as a café owner called Albert, had attracted the attentions of Messrs Croft and Lloyd.

'Jeremy came up with the *'Allo 'Allo* idea – and I immediately reckoned it was a brainwave,' says David. 'We had been working on a couple of ideas for shows to succeed *Are You Being Served?*

which was coming to an end. We worked on one idea for two days, got to page eighteen, and knew it would never work.

'Suddenly Jeremy had that flash of inspiration. It was always the TV programmes of that kind which were our targets – never what actually happened during the war. As soon as we started writing it we knew it was right – and we wrote the pilot in just a couple of days. When it is good it flows. Things do not necessarily get better because you spend longer on them.

'We knew *'Allo 'Allo* was a winner, and I think one of the reasons we got so much flak over it in the beginning was because we put it together rather well – we filmed it as if it were one of those drama series we were taking the mickey out of. Had we called it *Carry On Resisting* we would probably have got away with it.

'I think one of the reasons that the French have not been nearly as offended about the show as we may have expected, and why indeed they were prepared to buy it, is that they are probably more realistic about wartime resistance than we are.

'The number of people in the Resistance movement did swell dramatically during the last three months of the war in Europe, you know. And that was absolutely fair enough. France was well and truly occupied and that was something people had to learn to live with until they could effectively do something about it. The Resistance in some areas was regarded as a dangerous nuisance. They would kill two or three Germans, and thirty or forty French men and women would be executed in retaliation. I am sure if I had been living in France I would have wanted the Resistance movement kept under very tight control until it could really make a difference.

'I think some of the younger French in particular feel much the same about the stories they may have been told by grandmother, and there is not quite the reverence we may think.'

Seven years later *'Allo 'Allo* remains a success quite simply because it is funny. For the French to think so too – and to buy a British comedy show which makes them the butt of jokes set in the period of their greatest modern ordeal – is probably our programme's finest tribute.

Chapter 5

My Mum, My Dad and Me

One of the most difficult times of my life was when I confessed to my mother that I was homosexual. She was an old-fashioned conventional Yorkshire woman and she was dumbstruck. Then she cried, and about the first thing she said was: 'Don't tell your father. It will kill him.'

I don't know whether it would have done or not, but certainly nobody ever did tell my father. And if he ever suspected that I was gay, as I sometimes think he must have done, he never let on. My mum was different. We were very close. And there wasn't much I got up to that she missed.

I was twenty-two when she confronted me one day. I had a special friend who had stayed with us at home, and because of the way we had behaved together and how I was when he went abroad to work, my mother had a fair idea of the sort of relationship we had.

One evening she sat down and she said: 'I want to talk to you.'

'What about?' I asked her. I think I had a fair idea from the look of her. She was very serious. Very quiet.

'There's more than just a friendship between you two lads, Gorden, isn't there?' she said to me.

I tried to bluff it out. 'I don't know what you mean, mum,' I said.

But she wasn't having any of that. 'Oh yes you do,' she said. 'I just want you to tell me the truth. There is, isn't there?'

I was still hedging. 'Maybe,' I said. I could tell she wanted to know, although at the same time she was frightened of what she was going to hear. To her it was something out of another world. It was bound to be very difficult for a woman like her to understand.

In many ways, like in early 1989 when my sexuality finally became public knowledge, I was relieved to be given the opportunity to be honest. I was only reluctant to tell her because I knew it would upset her. But in the end I had to give her the truth, just like she asked for. It wasn't easy. She started sniffling and I sat by her on the arm of the chair and all that, and tried to comfort her. She was wonderful really. She tried to accept it. She indicated to me that if I had a special friend I should always bring him home, rather than go anywhere I might find myself in a compromising position.

But I know it took her a long time to get used to the idea that I was gay, and I don't know for certain if she ever really got used to it. I know she never mentioned it again. The subject was simply not discussed. It definitely shook the bond we had between us, but it couldn't break it. I don't think anything could ever have done that.

I was most aware of that bond, strangely enough, the day she died. I experienced something at exactly the moment she went, something weird. I have never spoken publicly about it before.

Mum was in hospital and I had been going to see her every day. But on the Thursday of that week I had the afternoon off work to go for an interview for what turned out to be my first job as a professional actor, with Bolton Rep.

On the Friday I went to work as usual in the sales office of this mill in Halifax, and there was a phone call from the hospital. 'Mr Kaye, your mother is not very well, we've had to put her on a ventilator. The heart's not very strong and we think you should come straight away,' I was told. So I got in my car and I drove to the tractor factory where my father worked and we went together to the hospital and we sat with mum. She was barely conscious, but they said she was settling a bit and she was stable.

It was mid-afternoon and I said to my dad: 'Look, I'll go home on the bus, I'll make some tea, and if you come later in the car, in about forty-five minutes, we'll have our tea, and then we'll set off together back to the hospital.'

So off I went to the bus stop. There was a bus that ran right in front of the hospital, but if I walked round the corner to the main road I could have a choice of three buses. There was no bus in sight outside the hospital, so I set off walking. It was August, yet there were already a few leaves on the ground. I remember that it was a sunny afternoon, a very pleasant afternoon, but I was feeling low as you can imagine.

Suddenly everything went very quiet. Just for a moment there was no traffic. No people. And it was a busy street, quite wide, tree-lined, with big Victorian houses on either side. I noticed this pile of leaves which were starting to move about even though there did not seen to be any wind. Suddenly they just whipped up off the pavement, all gathered together like a little tornado, and they whirled around my legs. They made this wooshing noise, like a kettle full of steam, wound themselves in a circle around my legs and then fell down again. I immediately looked at my watch, and it was exactly four o'clock.

It was such a peculiar thing. I felt the unease right away. I knew, I think, that it meant my mother had gone. I knew it meant something, anyway. But I didn't turn back. I just kept on going home according to plan. I behaved quite mechanically.

A bus came along and I got on it and went home. I carried on making the tea, getting things together as if I was expecting my dad to turn up for his tea about a quarter to five, five o'clock. But earlier than that the car drew up outside.

My dad got out and stood at the gate and we looked at each other and he said: 'We're on our own now, lad.'

The first words I said were: 'What time?' And he told me four o'clock.

It was no surprise, not any of it. I had known, really. Why else would I ask what time?

This story is absolutely true. I couldn't make it up. But I know my father always had difficulty understanding it.

It's like when you meet someone for the first time and you say to them, 'Where do you come from?' And just before they reply 'Worcester', or wherever, you know that is the place they are going to say. But you can't tell them because it would sound daft.

Anyway, I remember the night before my mother died I had said in my prayers that I realized she was going to go soon but, please, let me see her again before she does. I had seen her again, and as soon as that visit was over she left us.

I still feel she is with me sometimes. She was a typical Northern housewife with a very Victorian demeanour. She was small and dumpy, but she had actually been a very pretty lady when she was younger. Come to that, she was a very pretty lady when she was older. She put on a lot of weight with the years and she was a bit roly-poly. But she was always a delight.

My mother had been brought up very strictly by Victorian parents and she treated me the same way. I was brought up in a very old-fashioned way. Up until I was in my middle twenties she would wait up for me whatever time I came in. It didn't matter what time it was – there were no restrictions, I was free to come and go as I pleased – but she would never go to sleep until I was safely home. She would be upstairs, in bed more than likely, but wide awake, waiting, listening for the front door.

It used to be a bit of a game. I would come in really quietly, take off my shoes, creep into the kitchen to make myself a cup of tea or a mug of hot milk or whatever. Like a six-foot-tall, fourteen-stone mouse I was. But whatever I did I'd hear pad, pad, pad, her footsteps on the landing. And: 'Is that you, Gorden?' she'd call. Every time – 'Is that you, Gorden?'

I used to shout upstairs: 'No, it's a burglar. Go back to bed.'

And she would do just that, quite contented then, and fall straight off to sleep knowing I was safe indoors. She was like that all through her life right until the end – very possessive, very concerned about me.

My mum was an extremely emotional person and on one occasion she actually used tears to try to manipulate me. I remember the first day I left home when I was going to Bradford to live because I was about to do two plays in quick succession at the Bradford Playhouse – I was in the Bradford amateur drama group.

I had been working in Halifax and travelling there from Huddersfield in the mornings to do my job, then to Bradford to do my rehearsals, and home to Huddersfield late in the evening for my supper.

It was exhausting, and to begin with I used to have to go everywhere by bus. The problem was that I'm a terrible traveller on buses, especially late at night when I'm tired. I still get travel-sick on a bus or even in a car if I try to read, but then I was really bad. The buses ran every quarter of an hour from Bradford to Huddersfield and it was a forty-five-minute journey – sometimes I'd take three buses to do it because I would feel so ill I'd have to get off one bus and wait for the next one. Fifteen minutes on each was all I could stand.

It could take me some hours to get home on a bad day. So I decided to go and lodge in Bradford, which was all of eleven miles away. I think by the time I actually got it fixed I had managed to buy a car, but it still seemed like a good idea to cut down on all that travelling. I'd come home at weekends and it was only eleven miles, I kept telling mum.

It made no difference. I still remember her standing at the top of the stairs waving me off as if I was going to Timbuctoo never to be seen again. The tears were streaming down her face. 'My boy is leaving me,' she cried. All of that we went through. And I was twenty-two years old and moving half an hour's drive down the road.

I suppose, looking back, that I was quite restricted by my mother, but I wasn't aware of it at the time. I just took the way things were for granted. I didn't give in, though, about moving to Bradford. I knew it was important to give it a go. But I went back home after that, and one way and another I lived at home with my parents, and with my dad on his own after mum died, until 1979 when I eventually moved South to London. I was thirty-eight years old then.

One of my big regrets is that my mother never saw me become a professional actor. As I have already said, it was the day after my interview with Bolton Rep that my mother died. And the day before her funeral I learned that I had got the job, my very first professional acting job. Just a few days too late for my mother even to know about it.

She saw me as an amateur in Bradford many times – and it was a first-class amateur company too – but never as a pro.

My dad lived on another twelve years. And he did at least garner some slight notoriety at my expense and got pints of bitter bought for him on the strength of my being in *Coronation Street* – that sort of thing. He remained, however, completely un-stage-struck. At heart he was totally unimpressed. He was a great leveller.

I remember when I was in *The Street*, funnily enough, I brought a friend home for the weekend – a *Guardian* journalist called Derek who now works for the *Radio Times* and is still a great mate – and we were watching John Gielgud on television doing something really wonderful and emotive. The tears were flowing, and it was very moving.

Derek and I are just sitting there gobsmacked. We are totally in awe of this great actor who is weeping real tears in front of us. He is making us feel all that he is feeling and we both have a lump in the throat and we are just mesmerized by the power of the man.

My father, on the other hand, is totally unaffected by this brilliant performance. 'Turns it on just like a tap, dun't 'e,' he said.

Derek absolutely roared with laughter and has never forgotten it. Neither have I, come to that.

He was a tough old bird in more ways than one, my dad. Quite a creaking door regarding his health actually, but he would never give in to anything. He kept shocking the doctors with his resilience – a very resilient man he was. Once, when he was in hospital after his third coronary, his heart actually stopped. We all thought that was it and my Auntie Marjorie, my mother's younger sister who all the family relied upon, and I left him in intensive care in the morning and went home to discuss the funeral arrangements – who was going to do the catering, that kind of thing.

Anyway, we went back later and he was sitting up in bed saying, 'Hallo, Gorden, where have you been?'

He didn't know what had happened. I tried to tell him tactfully that he went away from us for several minutes. He didn't know what I was talking about. 'I'll 'ave to hit you over the head with a stick in the end,' I said to him.

But my mother had always been poorly. She had had polio as a child – infantile paralysis it was called then – and as a result she had very weak ankles. She was also arthritic, and she was diabetic. She didn't have to take insulin, but she had to watch the sugar levels and all of that. She had her worst ankle fixed when she was about sixty – had a metal pin put in it – and she came through that all right.

In spite of all her ailments she had a lot of fun out of life, and like all my family – Auntie Marjorie, whom I adored, and the whole lot of them – she loved a day out and she would never just sit in the car taking it for granted. She was always pointing things out and finding something to get excited about. Once I had my own car that was a great joy, and mum was a great one for setting off.

I would say: 'It's a nice day, shall we go out for a ride?'

And she'd say right away: 'Oh yes, just let me take my pinny off.' She'd take her pinny off and put on a bit of make-up and she'd be ready in seconds. She was never one of those who took two hours to get ready.

I remember when she collapsed and was rushed to hospital just before she died, she and my dad had just come back from the most glorious holiday. That was almost as if it was meant to be, too. At least they had that holiday, the pair of them. They'd taken my car and gone off touring and had a marvellous time.

It wasn't until then that I realized all of a sudden how much I loved her. You take it for granted, or most of us do, I think, that you love your mum and dad, but something has to happen, I reckon – illness or death or some other crisis – for you to give it any thought at all, really.

Anyway, I was so stunned seeing her as bad as she was that I passed out. I went to the hospital to visit her, and the family had warned me to prepare myself for a shock – that she wouldn't look in the best of health. But it didn't help. She was the colour of potted meat, and as soon as I saw her I fainted. It was a completely involuntary reaction – I just keeled over. So dramatic was my collapse that the nurses put me in an armchair, gave me a cup of tea and asked me if I would like a cigarette. Now that's quite something in a hospital. And I did indeed have a cigarette.

It's always been a point in my life that I have remembered vividly, because it was a purely emotional response, and a true emotional response is something you can do absolutely nothing about. It's like the way you feel about somebody. Even if they say, 'Don't feel like that about me,' you can't switch it off if it is a genuine emotion. It may be anger or hate or love, and it may be totally irrational, but if it comes from the heart you're stuck with it.

If it's love and you realize it's for the wrong person, like somebody you know feels nothing for you, you may be telling yourself continually that you really shouldn't feel that way, that you are going to be crapped upon from a great height. You can be quite clear about what is going to happen, your brain continues to operate quite independently and quite intelligently, but there is still nothing you can do about it. The feelings, whatever they are, remain. They may disappear with time – the great cliché that time is a great healer is right, of course – but you can't force it.

And when I saw my mother lying there and it dawned on me that she was dying, that the cheery, bright, kind person who had always been there for me was now in such a dreadful state – the floor just disappeared. I was a big lad in my mid-twenties, like I said, at least thirteen stone and six foot tall, and I went over like a ton of potatoes.

My father was a big man too, although as he got older he started to shrink a bit, as people do. I am quite like him physically and I know that I sound very like him – the same voice and accent.

The good thing about both of my parents was that they were very ordinary folk, Northern people without great educations, but they liked things, they enjoyed things, they were always excited about discovering anything new, and they were not afraid to express their appreciation. It was always a joy to take my mother out in the car, just as it was always a joy to take my dad out.

But there wasn't so much joy when he was teaching me to drive. It is traditional, of course, for families to fall out over driving lessons, and we were no exception. My father was a very strict teacher. When we were doing hill starts he used to take my watch away from me and tell me he had put it about a couple of feet behind one of the rear wheels. If I let the car run back it would crush my watch. I learned hill starts fast. Actually, looking back on it I wonder if he really did put my watch down on the road. But he certainly went through the motions.

He would come home from work, have his tea and then take me out in the car for an hour or two. But if I did anything wrong it was straight back home. There was one night when he ordered me home and we quarrelled quite badly. I wanted him to take me out again and he wouldn't have it and tempers were frayed. In the end I went off in the car myself for a couple of hours – to the horror of my mother. And I continued to drive on my own for about three months – I think it is safe to confess now after all these years – until I passed my test. I knew I was taking a stupid risk, but certainly there was no way my dad was going to relent and take me out, even though he knew how much I loved driving from the start. 'You wouldn't take my advice and that's that,' he said. He was a very stubborn man, my dad. And a very precise one, too.

I took him down to the South of France once because I had a friend in Yorkshire who had a caravan in St Tropez. Dad remembered every detail, everywhere we went, the exact route we took, everything we did, every meal we ate, and all the French place names even though he spoke no French, and he came home and related it all to the neighbours. Bored them rigid I shouldn't wonder. I was astounded with his grasp of it all.

Another time when he was recovering from one of his heart attacks I went to the doctor and said I would like to take him on holiday. He said that would be the best thing I could do provided it was somewhere warm. So I arranged to go to Majorca. I had never been there before.

We set off in the car across the Pennines on the M62 to go to Manchester Airport at 6 a.m. on this bleak November morning. The rain was horizontal and the wind was blowing, and I thought: 'I have flown in weather like this and I don't like it – what's he going to make of it?' I considered turning back.

When we got to Manchester Airport there were thousands of people all shouting and bawling; apparently there was a Spanish air controllers' strike. So what else is new? The outcome was that they could only fly us to Perpignan on the French–Spanish border. They couldn't fly us into Spain. There were three choices: we could cancel our holidays there and then, or they would drive us down to Torremolinos or Benidorm and put us up in a similarly priced hotel, or we could go to Palma in Majorca as planned. But continuing to Majorca would mean they would drive us from Perpignan to Barcelona, put us on the midnight ferry, and the journey would take twenty-two and a half hours instead of two and a half. And there was I with a sick man – well, a convalescing man.

I said: 'What shall we do, Dad? Shall we go back home?'

He was quite indignant. 'We're going to Majorca, son,' he said. 'We're off.'

I said: 'Dad, it's going to take forever.'

'Never mind that, we're off,' he said.

So we took off in this terrible weather and he thought it was wonderful. There he was, flying and eating sausage and beans – they gave us breakfast.

So we land in Perpignan and it's 65 degrees and the sun is shining and the weather is fantastic. There are a load of coaches that have brought people up from Spain and there are Germans and Scandinavians and English all milling about, and they load us in these buses and we drive down through Spain. We stop for lunch and it takes four hours because there are so many people. Eventually we get to Barcelona and it's about ten o'clock at night and there is this enormous ship looming up into the night.

The couriers did a remarkable job when you think about it, because there were people all shapes and sizes and nobody very happy about anything. We were still on the coach and they came around and said, 'We have cabin accommodation for mothers and children and for the elderly, and everybody else will have to fend.' They split the men and women up, four of each to a cabin, and they said they wanted me to go with my father because he wasn't so well. So we got the bags and carried them up this outside staircase, gasping for breath, and all the way down inside again. If we had been able to step right through the ship's side from the dock we would have been in our cabin.

There was my dad and these two elderly men we had been chatting to on the bus. I went and got them each a bottle of beer from the bar, and there they all were taking their teeth out and their glasses off and all of that. I had a top bunk and the fittest of the other two the other top bunk. So I got them all to kip and then I went up on deck.

At midnight the ship left and it was great. Then the dawn came up and it was absolutely beautiful. The sea was like a millpond. The sun rose behind the island and there was Majorca before us.

My father was tired, but then so was I, and after a few more hours' sleep at the hotel he was fine. I don't think he ever understood what I had been fretting about. We had the most wonderful holiday. As I said before, he loved plants and Majorca was paradise to him. There we were touring the island every day and when we saw a plant he didn't recognize, I had to stop the car we had hired while he conducted a scientific investigation. He'd dig them up to see if they grew from a bulb or a tuber or whatever, and then he'd plant them again. Wild plants they may have been, but he wouldn't just leave them by the side of the road, never. He would draw pictures and look things up in his gardening book when he got home.

Later on he had a hernia that they didn't want to operate on, so they gave him a truss. One morning he came downstairs and he could hardly walk. 'Are you in pain, dad?' I asked him.

'Oh, it's giving me jip this morning,' he replied.

He sat down, moaning. 'Have you got your pain killers?' I said.

He didn't know about that, and he stood up and he had this great lump at the back.

'What's that?' I said. 'Come on, take your trousers down.'

He had put it on back to front. He'd got this thing at the back that was supposed to hold the bits in. He got a little bit puddled as he got on, but he was still fighting fit.

When I moved down to London I had him down to live with me for a while. But it was a two-bedroomed flat and he never got used to not going upstairs to bed. I don't know what he would make of my home now – it's a kind of upside-down house. You actually have to go downstairs to be in two of the bedrooms.

My father finally died in 1980 just before we made *'Allo 'Allo*. So although he enjoyed twelve years of watching my career as an actor and maybe boasting a bit about what his boy was up to, he never saw me as René either. I think he and René could have been quite a double act.

Chapter Six

Only One O Level – But It Was French

I left school with just one O level GCE – and that was French. So appropriate it barely seems believable, does it? Perhaps I was preparing for René even then. I certainly gave few signs of preparing for anything else worth mentioning. I could have done better, I reckon. I was quite a bright boy at school, but I was lazy. Bone idle in fact.

I suppose there are a great many far more important and successful people than me in this world who could produce a schoolteacher to testify that he never believed they would amount to much. In my case I think there would be quite a number. Even at junior school I was beginning to discover that I could make people laugh, and I liked it. I was already learning to hide behind humour, to use it as a blanket which I could wrap right around my shyness.

I remember my parents being most distressed – my mother particularly – when they came home from a parents' meeting at my school. Apparently they had introduced themselves to my form master as Gorden Kaye's parents and he had replied: 'Oh yes, Danny Kaye we call him. A right little joker, that one.' He thought I was joking a bit too much and not getting on with my work, I suppose.

Anyway, in spite of that I managed to pass my eleven-plus. I was lucky enough, too, to get a reasonably high standard of pass, which allowed me to go to this old established top-stream grammar school, King James' in Almondbury. It was about three and a half, four miles out of the centre of town and about two and a half miles from where I lived – a bit of a bus ride. But it was set in the heart of this completely delightful, idyllic valley and is still a place that I go back to when I return to Yorkshire. It seems to draw me.

It was founded as a chantry school in the fourteenth century but it had a charter granted by King James I of England, King James VI of Scotland, in 1608. So when I was there in 1958 it was celebrating its 350th anniversary, and as it happens the charter had just recently been discovered. It was a glorious document, and is still kept there in a glass case with a screen over it so it doesn't deteriorate in the light.

To celebrate this event the school built a new cricket pavilion and invited various local dignitaries to open it. Well, I was in the fifth form by then, one of the older boys of seventeen. We were at an age where we were more than a little stroppy and anti any kind of establishment or conventionality.

The Countess of Scarborough and the Sheriff of York came in this great Daimler limo and drove around the perimeter of the cricket field, where we were all lined up in classes. And we were bidden to cheer and wave and make other respectful applauding noises while these high-up folk grandly swept by. Of course my bunch, young bolshy little yobs that we were, decided we would have no part in this. We greeted the limo with resounding silence, noses in the air, staring stonily ahead, and with a marked absence of clapping. We were summoned to the headmaster's study with alacrity. It was a place I grew to know well during my schooldays. I was certainly the resident japer all right.

Once I was responsible for putting drawing pins in the hammers of the piano in the school assembly room, which doubled as the gymnasium. We all filed in on this particular morning and the headmaster stood up on his rostrum and read out the hymn number: 'Fight the Good Fight' or 'Onward Christian Soldiers' – somehow it always seemed to be one of those two. Harry Gledhill, the music teacher, struck up on the piano and it sounded like somewhere between Mrs Mills and Winifred Atwell. There was this sort of jingling, jangling, plinkety plonk old Joanna rattling away at our very formal morning assembly in this ancient and hallowed grammar school. Not only were the boys' heads down, shoulders up, and shaking with laughter, but – to their credit, I now feel – so were the masters.

Unfortunately, however, this did not prevent the staff from winkling out the culprits of whom there were in fact several – although I believe I must confess that I was the gang boss of the King James Piano Mob. Yet another visit to the head's study.

I still consider my most legendary escapade, however, to be the case of the disappearing body. There was a new part to our lovely old school and the new buildings were, with breathtaking originality, known as N (for New) 1 and 2. Quite staggering. My class was in N2, which was on the first floor above the concrete school playground.

Now we had a very nervous, highly strung teacher, who, if we really tried, we could reduce to tears just by being bloody-minded. And being typically nasty little boys this, of course, gave us immense joy.

So this poor beleaguered chap, who really did not deserve us and was after all only trying vainly to bash some knowledge into our skulls, walked into my classroom to find a crush of boys crowded around the window crying: 'Hold on, for God's sake. No! No! Don't let go. Oh my God, he's gone,' etc. etc.

The teacher pushed forward and took in the spectacle of an empty pair of shoes in the hands of the boy nearest the window and me lying in a crumpled heap on the ground below. Exactly what we had banked on, happened. He did not give himself time to take in who was lying on the ground. He did not call out, 'Hey, you down there. Are you all right?' or anything like that.

As we had predicted, he immediately flew into a blind panic and ran screaming downstairs and out into the yard. As soon as he disappeared from the room my classmates shouted the all clear, and I dashed around the corner where my shoes were waiting for me and back to the classroom via another flight of stairs.

By the time the master returned, fuming and knowing he'd been well and truly had, I was in my correct seat and there was a full and attentive class, everybody sitting there quietly, everybody with their shoes on. This particular piece of mischief was most especially pleasing because I was never found out. Mind you, the teacher was so incensed that he kept us all in for two nights in any case.

However, that could have been a lot worse. It has to be remembered that my schooling took place during the heyday of that great symbol of the British education system – the cane. The trick was to pretend that you were not afraid of it and that you hadn't been hurt, but of course that was far from the truth. I remember one occasion when I was caught cheating with my French homework. It was not something I was in the habit of doing – honest – but somehow or other I had not done my homework by the time it should have been in, and it seemed like a good idea at the time to take somebody else's book from outside the staff room and do some quick copying.

With appalling timing I was just putting the other boy's book back in the pile when the French master came out of the staff room on his way to assembly. I had no chance. He said not a word, let me sweat until next French class, gave back my book in which was written 1/10 – come to think of it, I don't know why he gave me the one – and dispatched me to the head again.

We were getting to be quite good friends, the head and me. He was a great headmaster, as it happens. He always wore a gown – not the mortar, but always the gown. He appeared to be very bleak, very stern, but actually had a smashing sense of humour. He knew the story, of course, but made me tell him it and then asked how many marks out of ten I had been given. When I told him he just said he was going to give me three strokes of the cane. So I held out my hand and, as ever, was trying to keep back the tears until I got out of his door. I had nearly made it when he called out: 'Kaye.'

I turned around, desperate to leave.

'Next time, copy off somebody who can do it, all right?'

I remember even then with my hand feeling as if it were on fire, thinking suddenly it was all right again, there was humanity there in a funny sort of way.

One of my best pals at school was also a bit of a lad. His name was Chris Daley, and were he not a Yorkshireman he could well have grown up to become Arthur Daley in *Minder*. He was witty and good fun and sharp rather than clever. But one day he did something very clever indeed – at least, I thought it was. On his English report the master had written: 'Little improvement this term'. Now Chris was somewhat scared of his father, so he altered it to 'A little improvement this term'. But somehow or other he got found out and was sent to the head for the obligatory couple of whacks. When he returned, fingers burning, the English teacher looked up and said: 'Not little sympathy, Daley . . . but a little sympathy.' I always thought that was rather nice. There was the humanity again. And the humour. It was that kind of school.

I have a feeling Chris Daley was one of the young shockers involved in visits to a series of nude shows being staged at the local Palace Theatre. We were only fifteen or sixteen years old, but a group of us managed to get in on more than one occasion. Of course in those days the unclothed ladies were not allowed to move and so the curtain would go up and there they would all be in a kind of tableau with their top halves naked to the world. Our chief purpose in life was to force some kind of movement, and I recall that the use of pea-shooters played a large part in this.

One day we had a real treat. The show was called *Nudes in 3D*. Rather than the usual routine of the curtain being raised to reveal the naked ladies, a kind of conveyor belt had been constructed for this show which ran right up the centre aisle of the theatre. The girls stood on this conveyor belt in rigid pose, absolutely immovable, and were transported from behind a curtain right through the heart of the eagerly awaiting audience. I remember vividly that when about the fifth girl was thus travelling statuesquely up the aisle the conveyor belt failed to stop and reverse as it had previously.

Instead it kept trundling along and the poor girl simply toppled off the end of it and fell in a crumpled heap on the floor. Now she knew she should not move – and she didn't, either. She just lay there until a couple of burly minders came running with blankets which they threw around her before hustling her off backstage.

I must confess that we grammar schoolboys thought this was superb sport and were in hysterics for some days. The vision of that unfortunate girl pitching off the end of that silly conveyor belt is etched on my mind for ever.

Now I am sure *Nudes in 3D* was highly educational, but I do wish I had taken more advantage of my schooldays in other ways. I continue to feel I read the wrong books. I am still lazy. I'm bright enough, but I don't think I am particularly intelligent. I tend to read pulp for relaxation. I tuck into thrillers like Robert Ludlums and all those highly readable kinds of books which are like the movies I watch. They are manipulative, really – they excite your curiosity and lead you on. I feel I should be reading Macaulay and Harold Nicolson and those kind of people, but I don't. I find myself thinking that they are out of my league. And those kinds of thoughts are reflected in lots of ways. I suppose it is to do with my upbringing, not being able to get the working class out of me.

None the less they were happy times. And I did get that French O level specially for René.

Strangely, perhaps, I was never interested in appearing on stage at school, never one for the drama groups or any of that. That sort of thing wasn't me at all. I was so incredibly nervous of standing up in public that I only ever did one school play, and it still makes me squirm with embarrassment when I think about it. It was Shakespeare's *Henry IV*. I was Scroop, Earl of Masham, and I had to wear some particularly baggy tights. The whole thing was garbage, absolute garbage. Terrifying. And it was many years later before I actually gained the courage to venture out on to a stage again.

But off stage I was learning all the time to be a performer. I was getting really good at playing dead for a start. And more seriously there was the self-preservation bit. Having the squinty eye, and being overweight, with the tendency to blush in Technicolor if somebody's pet dog glanced in my direction, did make me a bit of a target at school. I wouldn't say I was exactly bullied, but I might have been had I not already discovered the sheer power of laughter.

A lot of comic actors will tell you that they started at school impersonating the teachers and entertaining their friends, coming out with a witty comment or the one-liner from the back of the class that would make the others laugh and result in you getting your earhole clipped. But this was the kind of behaviour that kept you out of any trouble with your mates. If you were going to be bullied or going to have your satchel thrown over the wall, you knew you could lighten the situation with a humorous quip. It was a great defence mechanism.

I became quite adept at wriggling out of all kinds of trouble, come to think of it. At getting my own way, really. I was not so good at sports, and I had no interest in getting hot and sweaty and uncomfortable in activities I did not enjoy. But I had a fairly quick mind on how to avoid sports. When it came to the cross-country runs I managed to get quite a few people on my side, and we would take short cuts and find places to hide and smoke cigarettes and come in gasping at the end, as if we had run the whole lot, when we had in fact done about two hundred yards.

Smoking became a bad habit of mine early on. But drinking was never to attract me. Naturally during my schooldays we would sneak off to a pub and try to pretend we were eighteen and order half pints of bitter. It was all bravado and I actually thought the stuff tasted like particularly unpleasant medicine – and I still do think that. But it took a long time before I dared to admit to myself, let alone anyone else, that I actually didn't like the taste of beer and I would much rather have a ginger ale. I got relentlessly teased at first. It was: 'Three halves of bitter and what will you have, Gorden? A rub down with a wet cloth?' But the novelty wore off after a bit and they left me alone. I always stood my corner, after all. Nothing has changed. I only ever drink wine to be polite and although I occasionally drink champagne I actually prefer it with orange juice, and just a fresh orange juice on its own would be my first choice every time.

Of course on special occasions I have been known to be led astray and to have a drink. The result is that I get drunk very easily. Some time after I had left school, but while I was still living at home with my mother and father, I went out to celebrate the homecoming of a friend called Keith Howell – the son of a neighbour who lived just across the street from us. Keith was in the RAF and had just returned from Singapore, where he had developed the habit of drinking strong ale with whisky chasers. I

Above; 'Legs and Co.!' Palladium, 1989.

Below; René's gesture says it all − the best gang in the world.

Left; On set with Hilary Bonner.

Right; Collecting the 'Tric' award for the best sit-com, 1987. *(Foto-Call)*

Below; Edith and me with the 'Boss', 1987.

Right; 'If you think I am eating that, you are out of your mind!' Thetford, 1987. *(Eastern Daily Press)*

Left; Three cowards on a wobbly roof. René prepares to leap into the unknown. *(Radio Times, photo by Don Smith)*

Below; Me on the set at Lynford Hall. All of the background is courtesy of the BBC design department.

The moment of truth. Eamonn Andrews says those four terrifying words, November 1986. The late and sadly missed Jack Haig is on the right.

'The Family' on *This is Your Life,* 3 November 1986, at the Prince of Wales Theatre.

Above; Usher at my cousin's wedding, 1954. My first long pants.

Above; Bridlington, 1963. You see, I was slim once!

Right; Dad and me at home, 1971.

Below; Me, Mum, Auntie May, Dad and cousin Joan at my cousin's wedding in Leeds, 1957. (Note the Brylcreem.)

Above; Hospital broadcast with Dave Clark…

…and Cliff Richard, *c.* 1963. *(Right)*

Below; As a bumbling disk jockey,
April Fool's Day, 1987. *(Vic Bennett)*

Above; Jeremy Lloyd and David Croft OBE. What would we do without them?

Left; With Bob Hope, 1984.

Below; As W.C. Fields at a fancy dress party, 1985.

Left; I lost my head in *King John,* 1986.

Below; As Audrey in *As You Like It* with Nigel Hawthorne, USA National Theatre Tour, 1974.

allowed myself to be persuaded to join in this lethal mix of tipples. Well oiled, we moved from pub to pub and finally to a dance at Huddersfield town hall, where in very high spirits we swept a number of young ladies around the dance floor.

By the time we tried to get ourselves home I was pole-axed. I was singing noisily and staggering so badly I could hardly stand. About a hundred yards from home the local policeman spotted us and said to me: 'Have you got far to go?'

Blind drunk and still trying to be funny, I replied: 'Don't be ridiculous! Can't you see this is the last waltz?' And I promptly knocked his helmet off. Slowly and with great dignity the policeman picked up his helmet, replaced it on his head and reached for his pencil and notebook. My friend Keith quickly explained that I lived just around the corner, that I was not used to drinking, and that he would take me home right away.

The policeman very generously replaced his pencil and notebook in his inside pocket and said to Keith: 'Just get him out of my sight.'

The strange thing is I remember waking up in the morning with no ill effects at all and spotted Keith wearing sunglasses and sitting in the shade in the little garden opposite, nursing a monumental hangover. So it is not the morning after that frightens me—but to this day I can get quite tipsy on one large glass of wine.

I think one of the reasons why I may not have tried as hard as I should have done at school was that about halfway through my grammar school days I realized that my parents could not afford to send me to university even if I were clever enough to get there. In Huddersfield there was a choice of three industries – textiles, chemicals or engineering. So I went into the sales office of a textile mill, John Crowther's, at Milnsbridge.

We were very proud of our skills in Huddersfield, and I remember that John Crowther's held the record for taking wool from a sheep's back and putting it on to man's back. They brought sheep to the mill, where they were shorn. The wool was washed and scoured and then carded, which is a process it goes through to get all the fibres in line. It was then spun and woven on a loom into a three-and-a-quarter-yard length of fabric, which is a gentleman's suit length. This fabric was then scoured and finished and inspected. A tailor standing by measured the managing director, cut out the suit, stitched it up and had him dressed in it in three hours thirty-seven minutes.

When James Callaghan was Prime Minister he had some cloth woven in Huddersfield with a stripe in it, which if you studied it closely was formed of the letters JC. There were two suit lengths and he had one made into a business suit for himself, and took the other as a present for Jimmy Carter when he was President of the USA, because of course his initials were JC too. And I took as much pride in that as anybody who was ever involved in the textile industry in Huddersfield.

I was interested in my work from the beginning, and I do not recall being bored. I recall being bored at school speech days, though – and in fact those occasions are my worst memories of school. They used to be held in the evenings in Huddersfield Town Hall, which is very splendid and is where Huddersfield Choral Society sings. There is a big organ with great pipes. But in those days nothing helped the dreadfulness of speech day. We used to have this wonderful teacher, George Beech, who every year would teach you to stand up quietly in unison – you don't stand up by banging your feet, he would say. Speech day used to be purgatory. Those speakers really had been trying, they were so deadly dull. And we boys would have to give up an evening, in return for which the speaker would ask for half a day's holiday. Then, if you were lucky maybe, if you'd been particularly good at sports perhaps, you would get chosen to be given a whole day.

But whatever you got, you still had to suffer speech day. And I made a promise that in the unlikely event that I was ever invited back to speak I would be wild and outrageous and totally anarchic because of the poor kids who had to sit through it.

Happily, in 1988 I was invited back. I have to admit with some lurking shame that I was not at all anarchic. I was actually quite proud to be there. And I had to follow the Deputy Chief Constable of Yorkshire, who turned out to be very good and very funny, so maybe the standard has improved since my day.

I simply apologized for René being unable to be there because he was working on a new series at Elstree, but said that he had sent a letter which I would read. And although anarchy is far too strong a word I did get my revenge a bit for all those bloody boring hours I had to sit through with dreary school governors rabbiting on. I gave them two pages of René on the horrors of speech days, and it seemed to cause some amusement.

Mind you, I think the school got its own back on me too. They gave me a nice picture in a frame – it turned out to be that French O level GCE certificate which I had never even bothered to pick up at the time. Perhaps I should ask the BBC if we could display it on the walls of the Café René.

Chapter Seven

Eamonn and Noel

One of my most wonderful experiences was being chosen as a subject for *This Is Your Life*. It was a very special day, and I only wish my parents had lived to share it with me.

I am inclined to kid myself that I'm terribly on the ball and see things coming a mile off. But Eamonn Andrews and his team from Thames TV got me cold. Targets of *This Is Your Life* are always being asked if they had any idea what was about to happen – the inference is: surely you must have had a suspicion. Well, I can assure you I did not have a clue.

Eamonn made his hit at the Prince of Wales Theatre just as the first West End run of *'Allo 'Allo* was beginning there in 1986. A message went up on the stage door notice board that Thames TV wanted to record clips from the show for a programme about comedy in the theatre and on television – about the things which make people laugh. We were told we would be a small part of an hour-long documentary to be called *It's a Funny Business*.

I arrived at the theatre – as I always do – at about 6.15 p.m. so that I could park my car and have plenty of time to relax before curtain up. Sam Kelly, Captain Geering on stage then and for the first three TV series, always used to get in early too, and when I popped my head in his dressing room to say hello he said he was going for a bowl of soup at a little café called the Stockpot. So I joined him, and as we walked past the back of the theatre there was the Thames TV van. I just remarked: 'Oh yes, they are doing those inserts tonight, aren't they?' and thought no more about it. Now Thames is quite a small outfit where everybody knows everybody else. There are only about four Thames crews, and it was quite possible that I might pop my nose into the van to pass the time of day. So would you believe that there were actually captions in the van saying *It's a Funny Business*, and various bits of highly visible evidence which would instantly copper-bottom their cover story – just in case.

Completely unawares I went on stage and played René, and of course at the end of the show, when we are all bowing and waving and bowing some more, the curtain didn't come down. I'm thinking, 'Come on, we're finished now, we've got a packed house and it's been great but let's not hang about, let's not make a meal of it, let's get home.' Suddenly a great roar goes up from the audience. I look to the left and there is this figure trotting along dressed in an airman's hat and a flying jacket and clutching a microphone. It is Eamonn Andrews.

I remember very clearly and instantly thinking that he must be doing Jack Haig's life – because Jack must have been in the business more than sixty years. And then I thought, 'No, if they were doing Jack's life I would have known about it.' By the time the obvious explanation began to dawn upon my numbed senses Eamonn was right there in front of me and I was completely flummoxed.

They actually did the show there and then, at 10.30 at night in the Prince of Wales Theatre – which was a first, apparently. They usually whisk you off to the studio or somewhere, where everything is all set up. But they decided to try and do it the other way around, and they had brought a special audience of 150 of my friends and family to the Prince of Wales. Then there was this wonderful moment when they told the theatre audience that if anybody would like to stay they would be welcome and Thames would be very grateful, but of course some would have buses and trains to catch and would have to go, and would they please leave right away. The show would be starting in twenty minutes. To everyone's astonishment only about forty out of twelve hundred people left. That meant the invited audience couldn't find anywhere to sit.

There were people standing at the back of the theatre. It was bloody marvellous.

I went upstairs to my dressing room and there was my agent, who was positively gloating, and all these wicked folk who had known all along, looking smug. And there was a bottle of champagne waiting for me. I was allowed to change into my clean white shirt and freshen up a bit, and Eamonn talked to me for just about the full twenty minutes before the show and completely relaxed me. He really was a fabulous man. I remember me prattling on about taking the show to New Zealand the following year when I would be able to see all my relatives over there whom I had never met, and you might have thought, knowing the format of the programme, that I could have had just a fleeting idea that the New Zealand relatives might be brought over. I promise you it never entered my head – not even, particularly not, in fact, when Eamonn showed filmed footage of them in New Zealand. Then they walked on stage and it was a great moment.

My mother's elder brother John married a girl from Stoke-on-Trent and emigrated to New Zealand in 1911. It must have been one hell of a brave thing to do to take off in those days to the other side of the world to start a new life for yourself. It took weeks to get there by sea, and they would have known little of the country that was to be their home – there was no television beaming into their front rooms to show them what it looked like. And in the days before air travel and the telephone made it smaller, our planet was a big and mysterious place. But Uncle John, just twenty-three years old, and his young bride settled down well and had five children, three sons and two daughters.

One of the sons died very young, but three of my first cousins, all in their seventies, are still alive – Jean, Margaret and Russell. They were all brought to England for *This Is Your Life*, two of them with their spouses. I now have a family of forty in New Zealand, and it was on *This Is Your Life* that I first met any of them.

Apparently when the Thames researchers telephoned my seventy-six-year-old cousin Jean to invite her over she didn't believe a word of it. A voice said: 'Are you Mrs Jean Sullivan? We believe you are Gorden Kaye's cousin, and this is Thames TV and we are going to do a *This Is Your Life* on him in London and we'd like you to come.'

Jean was convinced it was a hoax and replied in direct fashion: 'Oh, get away. Who is this?'

But it happened. It was quite a night. My relatives joined with the celebrity guests like Jess Conrad, Frank Ifield, Susan Maughan and Christopher Timothy – who brought a piglet in memory of my guest appearance on *All Creatures Great and Small* when I played a pig farmer who couldn't bear to kill his favourite pig.

The real star of the show, however, was my beloved Auntie Marjorie, my mother's younger sister, who sadly died about a year later. Auntie Marjorie was a cracker. Frank Ifield appeared to fall in love with her. It was actually one of the biggest surprises of all having Auntie Marjorie there and looking so perfectly at home, because she was getting very frail and had hardly been out anywhere for ages. In fact the last outing had been not long before, when we had taken the show to the Alhambra Theatre, Bradford, and she had been brought by car to see us. Apparently the Thames people were already up North researching and were terrified that I might bump into them. They visited Auntie Marjorie four or five times and she put them right on a number of things. She always was the family chronicler. And I might have guessed she would not have missed *This Is Your Life* as long as she could draw breath. It certainly would not have been the same without her.

She tricked me rotten over the weekend when she came down to London to rehearse and go through everything with Thames. I always used to phone her on Saturdays or Sundays, so she called me first with some cock-and-bull story about how she wouldn't be in because she was going off with my cousins, Nora and Alec, who were going to take her for a run in the country. Dumbly, it never struck me that was not very likely as it was November and the weather was sure to be foul in Yorkshire. Anyway, down to London she came and took to it all with the greatest of ease, saying her piece on television with no trouble at all, not fluffing a single line. And, of course, when she got back to her little mill cottage in the village of Kirkheaton outside Huddersfield she was an eighty-five-year-old TV star, which she absolutely revelled in.

There was one rather disconcerting thing about it all. The show was recorded on Monday, 3 November and broadcast on Wednesday, 5 November 1986. And on 5 November 1987 Eamonn died. Exactly a year later. Slightly creepy, really.

I had the greatest possible admiration for Eamonn. I had appeared on one *This Is Your Life* before my own – for Rodney Bewes – and it was then that I first realized what a top-to-toe professional Eamonn was. Michael Aspel is absolutely first-rate, of course, and did a superb job of following somebody almost impossible to follow, but I think he would be the first to admit that Eamonn was extra-special.

He had a way of making it look so easy. He would appear to be quite ordinary and putting no effort into anything – and yet all the time people would be counting him down into film. There is so much to think about in that show, because usually it is done straight through in one take and it has to work like clockwork. I thought it was just miraculous that he could maintain his rather man-in-the street attitude while all this was going on. And also to his credit I believe the pleasure he appeared to take in other people's enjoyment was absolutely genuine and not put on at all.

I remember when he was walking me to my dressing room before my own show that I said to him: 'What a way to earn a living, scaring the pants off people.' Now Eamonn never forgot anything – not even a flip remark made to him at a time like that. When he sent me the famous big red *This Is Your Life* book he had written in the front: 'What do you mean, scaring the pants off people? All very best wishes, Eamonn Andrews.' I treasure it.

Funnily enough, the Bradford Alhambra where I was playing when Eamonn and the team started work on my *This Is Your Life*, was also the scene of another telly trick which was played on me. We were approached by the BBC allegedly to do a live insert for John Craven's *Newsround*, in which Carmen Silvera and I were to talk about the refurbishment of the Alhambra Theatre which had just had £8¼ million spent on it. An interviewer called Nigel Farrell came up to Bradford and explained that he wanted us to go on and talk about the play a little bit, and that they would then show shots of the theatre and we would discuss what had been achieved. We rehearsed it and prepared to shoot on stage, and the idea was that we would sit in the Café René drinking coffee together. We rehearsed at 4.30 and I was told we would be on live at 5 p.m. and they counted us into the programme.

Nigel Farrell began the transmission talking to camera in front of the curtain, which was down, and Carmen and I were sitting behind the curtain watching a monitor while they showed some pan shots of the theatre. Then the curtain rose and Nigel said that now appearing in this lovely theatre was the highly successful stage version of the TV comedy hit *'Allo 'Allo* and here were two of its stars.

He came and joined us, and asked Carmen a question, and then he turned to me and asked me about the differences between appearing on TV and on stage – and as I began to answer he spilt his coffee on his trousers. The whole of the cup went into his lap and it was scalding, and he was silently screaming and jumped instinctively to his feet.

Now, you have to remember at all times during this story that I am convinced we are going out live on television. So, from the corner of my eye I can see from the monitor that the camera is firmly on me. I think, as long as it stays there, we're all right. I am also aware of this poor man, with hot coffee burning his vital parts, writhing in agony. A little to my surprise he took his trousers off and started mopping himself up around the area of his boxer shorts. I keep on talking – desperately. Goodness knows what I was saying, but I did not dare pause for breath. Then the floor assistant came along with some ice which was thrown over him and somebody else squirted foam at him. I carried on talking.

Just as it began to dawn on me in my state of frantic verbal diarrhoea that there was slightly excessive behaviour going on, the truth was revealed. I had been made an unwitting stooge for Noel Edmonds's *Whatever Next* show, in which a *Candid Camera*-type trick like this was a regular spot. They had set the whole thing up just to see how I would cope under these kind of circumstances. There had, in fact, been a hidden camera behind my shoulder photographing all that was going on. And when the sequence was eventually shown on Noel's show the clip was stopped just before Nigel spilt his coffee, and two competing couples in the studio had to guess what happened next.

Once again, I was well and truly had. I don't know that I have ever really forgiven my very good friend Carmen Silvera for her part in that one. She, of course, had known all along, and happily watched me struggling.

Chapter Eight

The Beatles and the DJ

If I didn't still have the tape of the time I interviewed the Beatles I would probably think I had dreamed it. There I was, a shy over-weight, twenty-three-year-old office boy, virtually struck dumb with nerves, doing a radio interview with the Beatles in 1964 when they were at the height of their glory.

They had each just been given the MBE and had performed at their first *Royal Variety Show* – the famous one where John Lennon got a laugh out of the Queen Mum by telling the guests in the royal box to rattle their jewellery. They were about to go to America for that legendary Shea Stadium concert and all that followed it. They were riding very high. And I was in their dressing room doing my impression of Alan Freeman. This really was the big time.

You see, our local cinema used to stage live pop gigs occasionally. And in spite of everything I was by then well established as a disc jockey and interviewer with the local hospital radio station in my spare time. I and another amateur DJ called Laurie Stead used to try to interview all the stars who appeared at the cinema. Then, to the joy and amazement of every youngster in town, they actually got the Beatles booked. They were the biggest thing that had ever been to Huddersfield, and Laurie and I were quite determined to get them on our hospital radio.

We wrote to their manager, Brian Epstein, well in advance, asking for an interview, and somewhat to our surprise the answer was yes. It was a great coup, and to this day I am as proud of it as almost anything I have achieved – not because it was a particularly wonderful interview, but because we got in there. I was actually invited into their dressing room to talk to them.

Normally there were two of us on every interview – we worked as a team and would take it in turns, one to operate the recording machine and one to do the talking. Fortunately it was my turn actually to do the interview, because we were told that only one of us could go backstage. That meant I had to do it alone. I was very nervous and excited. But I got through it somehow and I had a perfectly presentable interview with the Beatles on tape.

I must say they did give me a tough time. They sent me up gutless. There were nine of them in there, so I was rather up against it – the four of them and five of their roadies. They were having a lot of fun, and some of it at my expense. But they were very good. They were witty and charming. Laurie did all the background stuff, interviewing people outside, and we built up a good programme.

Afterwards I wrote an article about it for the technical college magazine whose drama group I had by then joined. I had been told I must submit this article to Brian Epstein for his approval. I did so and he found fault with only one thing. I had described Paul McCartney as 'tall, dark, and O level English'. The word came back that I should change that to 'tall, dark, and A level English.' I still laugh about that.

I don't laugh so much when I play the tape back nowadays. I am acutely aware of my very droning Northern voice going on and on, all on the same note. And on my really bad days I wonder if anything much has altered over the years. But, regardless of my drone, it wasn't bad, and the lads recorded a message for Christmas as well. Funny, they did all the things I do now when I am asked to go on hospital radio as a guest.

One way and another that stint with the hospital radio was a most important part of my life. I'm not sure I would have been able to cope with any of the things that followed without all that wonderful experience. It did me so much good, it really did.

You see, the thing about me as an introverted lad was that I secretly didn't want to be like that. I hadn't enough confidence even to say so publicly, but I did say it to myself, and it was the absolute truth. I wanted something that would force me to be outgoing and extrovert. So there I was, this painfully shy kid hating myself, utterly loathing myself for my shyness, nineteen years old and desperate to change myself. I suppose nowadays I would be heading for a psychiatrist's couch, but such things didn't figure much where I was brought up.

I had been working in the sales office of this textile factory since I was seventeen. I had lots of spare time and I had a good job earning £4 7s 6d a week. I would give it all to my mum and get a bit of spending money back. I didn't have a car then, of course – I had a bike which I used to ride to work.

It was in the Colne Valley, the place where Harold Wilson was born. There are only two famous Huddersfield people, Harold Wilson and James Mason, and that's it. (I must say I do remember the first occasion the *Huddersfield Examiner* referred to me as *the* Huddersfield actor Gorden Kaye instead of *a* Huddersfield actor. The use of the definite article was a big moment.)

As I said before, I worked in John Crowther's textile mill, the one that had the three-hour thirty-seven-minute record for turning a sheep into a suit. I think it has all changed now, but in those days it was the only factory of its type that took the raw wool at one end and turned out the finished cloth, and, if necessary, the dyed cloth. They would dye the yarns and weave the cloth. That's one fabric process. Or they would weave plain cloth and dye that in the dye house. One day I was talking to the dye house supervisor and saying that I had all this spare time and he said: 'Have you tried hospital broadcasting? They are always looking for someone to help out. You should get in touch with the Lions, who run it.'

Now that immediately appealed to me, because I had always been a great fan of films and radio and that little upstart television. I already knew that I loved the world of entertainment and everything about it, but the thought of actually doing it, of becoming a part of it, had never crossed my mind. In fact the memory of that one school play could well have been the end of my showbusiness career before it began. I did after all, very nearly die of shame.

The Lions welcomed me eagerly, and I just went along originally to sort out the records and make lists of what should be played. Then someone said: 'Go on, you introduce the next record.' I didn't have time to duck out, and that was the beginning.

Radio at whatever level was and still is a wonderfully cosy, relaxing medium. It's very personal, somehow, a kind of cocoon to be in really. It never seems as if there is a big audience out there when you are sitting in a little radio studio.

And I knew my music. I was one of those lucky people who lived right through the rock and roll era. I was old enough to understand Bill Haley and Elvis Presley and then the amazing success of the Liverpool sound – Gerry and the Pacemakers, Freddy and the Dreamers, and of course the Beatles.

Now the worthy members of the Lions were mainly gentlemen of mature years and they were really running their radio for the older people in hospital, the homes for the blind and the elderly, and the old Huddersfield Royal Infirmary. But also being served was the TB hospital at Bradley Wood and then the new Royal Infirmary, and there were quite a lot of young people going into hospital who received the programmes too. So Laurie and I, who were both in our early twenties, realized there was a market other than for Kathleen Ferrier and Peter Dawson, the kind of fare they were playing, as well as the local news from the local papers read out for the blind. We went around to the hospital and got requests from the younger people and livened the music up, making it more popular. When I say popular I'm talking Mantovani, mind you – although occasionally we did have the Beatles or the Beach Boys.

Then there were the stars of the live pop concerts at the local cinema whom we would talk to. Cliff Richard, Billy Fury, Helen Shapiro, Frank Ifield and Rolf Harris were among our victims. I interviewed Helen Shapiro when 'Walking Back to Happiness' was a big hit, and I remember asking her if Helen Shapiro was her real name, which I suppose was a pretty dumb question. She replied very neatly: 'Would anyone change their name *to* Helen Shapiro?'

I also interviewed Ken Dodd and in 1988 we met up again on a rather more professional basis at the Children's Royal Variety Show. I reminded him of it. It was twenty-five years ago, but I still have a copy of that and I ran one off for him.

72

Another thing we did with the hospital radio was to try to bring the feel of Huddersfield to the listeners in the various hospitals and homes for the elderly and the blind. There used to be wrestling bouts sometimes in the town hall – scene of those dreadful school prizegivings I have already talked about – and a special ring would be built. We had a commentator who knew a lot about wrestling, and I used to go along and help set up the microphones and so on – it was all pretty much a do-it yourself job.

There was a particularly impressive display when a man called Harold Sakarta – who used to play Oddjob in the Bond movies and wrestled under the name of The Great Tojo – was top of the bill along with Mick McManus. He came along in a kimono walking on those great wooden blocks Japanese style, with his hair tied back, and he would scatter salt to each side of the ring to ward off the evil spirits. It was a wonderful piece of showmanship. Then he would take off the kimono and the audience would obligingly boo and hiss, and on would come Mick McManus and he would pull on the ropes and they would boo and hiss him as well, and the two would proceed to tear each other limb from limb.

The referee would try to clean the bout up while the Great Tojo went totally Japanese on him and with much Ah So-ing and bowing and and all of that, would pretend not to understand a word of English, while McManus made it clear he didn't care anyway. There were the usual yells of excruciating agony and threats of dismemberment, and the night was filled with hatred and violence.

I don't recall who won. I think they were probably both disqualified for appalling behaviour. Anyway, the crowd were on their feet booing and shouting and having a wonderful time and everybody went home filled with that warm glow that wrestling crowds get from watching two men apparently trying to kill each other.

We stayed on to de-rig and pack up our equipment and witnessed Harold Sakarta and Mick McManus coming out of the Mayor's Parlour, which had been used as their changing rooms, and walking together down the broad carpeted corridor of this Yorkshire town hall. The monstrous Sakarta was wearing a blue blazer and grey flannels and mad Mick McManus was dressed in a perfectly tailored dark suit.

And then I heard the Great Tojo, who of course spoke no English at all in the ring, say to his bitter opponent in beautiful Oxford English: 'I'm just driving over to Manchester. Would you like a lift?'

And McManus replied most politely: 'No, thank you very much. I have my own car with me.'

So there you are. They had done their performance, and it was just like actors leaving the theatre. As when René comes off stage and takes off his apron after he is finished for the evening, and Gorden puts on his overcoat, gets in the motor car and drives home.

It gave me a slight jolt to see that, and made me realize what skill there must be in wrestling. Judged on what I saw that night, they are as much performers as any actor. And performing was what I was learning all about. It's strange the things that make us what we are. I reckon you carry on learning right through your life, but that was a very special time for me.

I never had any formal acting training at all. What I know I learned on my feet. My understanding of my trade is seat-of-the-pants stuff. I am very lucky, I think, that God gave me a gift. I know that if I have funny lines to say the timing is instinctive for me. And timing is the single most important ingredient in comedy.

It was the local technical college drama group which provided me with my first theatre experience, and that was through a hospital broadcasting friend called David Coldwell whom I met up with again many years later when he appeared on my *This Is Your Life* programme. David was a student and already a member of the college group, and he had been trying for some time to persuade me to go along with him and at least become involved in something like operating the curtains or painting the scenery. He assured me that it would be great fun, and eventually I agreed to go with him one night when the group were rehearsing a play called *Marching Song* by John Whiting.

But David played a trick on me which turned out to be a vital ingredient in the shaping of my career. He was playing the role of an American film director in *Marching Song*, and I was supposed just to be watching the proceedings. But in fact David had that day received acceptance of his application to go to teachers' training college in Birmingham. When we arrived at rehearsals, he announced this in front of the producer and the entire cast and said: 'So I shall not be able to do the play after all – but my friend Gorden Kaye here will do it instead.'

I was flabbergasted. 'I couldn't possibly do it,' I cried in some state of fright. 'I'm just here to pull the curtains and move the scenery around, that's all.'

'Don't be ridiculous,' said David. 'You'll be fine.'

And the director, who was probably a little desperate come to think of it, joined in the reassurances, handed me the script and said: 'Just go on up and we'll see what you can do.'

So I stepped on to the stage of the hall in this technical college. It was just a platform, really, with a pair of curtains, no wing space and doors going into a back room. I started to read, and when I paused the director said that I was fine.

I began to relax a little and try to imagine that I really was an American film director. Then a funny thing happened. The hall was more or less empty, of course – it certainly was not the London Palladium – and I know it is easy to embroider a moment like this, but I honestly began to feel something stir inside me. It seemed as if I was meant to stand there high above the floor delivering lines. I began to enjoy it. I began to feel that I had found the place I was meant to be. So I played the part of this American film director and then went on to act in other productions for the technical college and to develop my love of comedy and to write and perform in rag reviews.

But meanwhile, as I became more and more excited by the sheer exhilaration of performing both on the radio and in the theatre, I still had a living to earn. I had four full-time jobs as an office worker in industry before I became a professional actor. I worked in two textile mills, a British wine factory and a tractor factory. The hospital radio work was all voluntary, of course, and I did that because I enjoyed it so much. But I also supplemented my income with a Saturday job in a local tailors, Montague Burton's in Huddersfield.

One of my jobs as the lad in this store was to take down a

customer's measurements called out by the experienced tailor. He would set to work with a tape measure and I would just have to fill in a standard form. It could be quite an amusing exercise, because there is a secret code of expressions which are used to describe somebody's figure so as not to insult him. I can still remember some of them. You see, you may have a forty-two-inch chest but you could also have a big belly, in which case the measurer would call out 'portly'. My favourite one was 'prominent seat' which was usually abbreviated to 'PS' and quite simply meant big bum. Well, you could hardly stand there calling out 'big bum', could you – hence the tactful abbreviations.

There is the old apocryphal story in the rag trade that if the sleeves are a bit long you tell the customer they will ride up with wear, and if they are a bit short you say they will ride down with wear. As the good menswear shop assistant you always have an answer. And years later when I appeared in *Are You Being Served?* I knew a lot of the lines. And so even my Saturday job did its bit towards preparing me to be a comedy actor and eventually to become René Artois.

Chapter Nine

Dangerous Moments

Had I ever been in the army I might have learned the importance of not volunteering. But I can never quite stop myself. Thus it was upon my own insistence that I was once chased three times across a football field in an episode of *Minder* by a super-fit Dennis Waterman. I did not expect to live.

I had been hired to play another minder, the bodyguard of a small-time villain. Arthur Daley had gone into hospital to have an ingrowing toenail removed, or something equally critical, and I was sent around in the middle of the night to put the frighteners on him, as Terry would say. It was all very moody. I had to walk down this long, darkly lit corridor, open the door to Arthur's ward and stand silhouetted in the doorway. I threatened Arthur with terrible retribution if he did not take heed of what I was saying, but naturally Terry got to hear of this. I was just about to do something really nasty to Arthur when, naturally, our Tel came darting in and, through a sequence of events I can no longer quite chronicle, I ended up being slammed against a goalpost by the young hero.

The plan was that Terry should knock nine bells out of me, and the fight arranger, Peter Braham, said: 'Look, Dennis has been in *Minder* and *The Sweeney* for so long that he is as good as any stuntman, but I don't want you getting hurt so I have got you a double, a lad called Del Baker.'

Well, even I had the brains to realize I could not cope with the kind of fight sequence that was about to happen. I had a beard at the time, so they gave Del a false beard and plonked a woolly hat like the one I was wearing on his head. He was about the same size as me and he looked fine. But, oh no, I could not just let him get on with it. I knew that before my character got beaten to a pulp he had to be chased by Tel across this football ground. Now although I am not built for speed, like many chubby people I am reasonably light on my feet (if not other people's) and I thought I could at least do my own running.

It was suggested to me tactfully that I might not in fact be able to run quite as fast as Dennis. 'I probably can,' I replied with wounded pride. So that was it. They put Dennis twenty yards behind me and called a rehearsal run. I set off across this field like a rather large greyhound for 150 yards or so and Dennis couldn't catch me. I can in fact run quite fast for short distances, but I had overlooked the probability of more than one take being required.

So now I'm feeling quite pleased with myself. Then another camera rehearsal is called, with me given slightly less of a start. This time Dennis catches me at approximately the right point and we prepare to film. Now I have run three hundred yards flat out and I am seeing stars and I am wishing I had kept my mouth shut, because soon I am going to have to run the length of this field – which is beginning to seem about as big as Wales – all over again. My chest is heaving painfully, and as the whole situation is entirely my own fault I am trying desperately not to show just how close I am to collapse.

Once, while appearing years and years ago in the first thing I ever did for Yorkshire TV, a series called *The Flaxton Boys*, my habit of volunteering for stuntwork nearly caused somebody else an injury. I was supposed to be a police driver of a motorbike and sidecar. I could not actually ride a motorbike so they used a stand-in. The idea was that they would shoot me getting on to the motorbike and then film the stand-in from the back. Well, of course, I said: 'Look, if you give me ten minutes I'm sure I can probably learn to ride the thing so that the director is not forced to do rear shots he probably does not want to do.'

They let me have a go. All went well until I had to drive straight towards the camera and stop quickly. We were on wet grass, I misjudged the whole thing and we did not stop nearly quickly enough. My passenger's head ended up in the focus box of the camera and it could have been very unpleasant. Fortunately, the cameraman had seen that I was about to make a mess of it and not stop in time and he dived off the camera out of the way.

Of course, nobody was all that worried if the bit part character actor gave himself a coronary through running too fast or broke his leg falling off a motorcycle. But when you are a central character in a hit TV show you are a little more valuable. The whole programme and a lot of people's jobs and futures depend upon you. But even as René in *'Allo 'Allo*, I still have this ridiculous urge to do as many of my own stunts as possible. And it is not as if I am the greatest athlete who ever lived, either.

David Croft and I have continual tussles over it. He gets quite angry and says: 'What if I lose you? What am I going to do if you get your legs broken?' Never mind my legs, but what about his programme, is the inference. Then he says: 'You are just like Arthur Lowe. He always wanted to do the bloody dangerous stuff.'

So I get compared with Arthur, and that I take as a wonderful compliment because I think Arthur Lowe was one of the greatest comedy actors who ever lived. David, however, is not trying to be nice to me – he is trying to get some sense into my head.

Once, in an early episode of *'Allo 'Allo*, there was a sequence where a runaway coffin which is supposed to be laden with bombs careers out of control on a little truck down a hill. It was held by fine guide-wires which the viewer couldn't see. Virtually the entire French cast chased after this coffin, because we were afraid it would explode at the bottom of the hill.

I said to David: 'I know, I'll jump on it. Let me jump on it. It will be funnier. Please let me.'

'No fear,' said David. 'What if you fell off? What if the bloody thing tipped over?'

I remember actually pleading with David until, totally exasperated he said: 'Look, we employ experts to do things like that. If I wanted René to jump on the coffin, I would call in a stuntman who looked like you to do so.'

None the less, he practically had to restrain me physically. On another occasion he did let me get my own way, and as usual I lived to regret my rashness. In one episode there was a scene involving an escape from a prisoner-of-war camp. We had a see-saw with Sam Kelly as Captain Geering on one end, and I was supposed to jump from the roof of a hut on to the other end. A fake roof had been built which was about six feet high – it was actually just a curve – and I was filmed jumping from that on to a pile of mattresses. Meanwhile a couple of tumblers out of *Barnum*, the Michael Crawford show about the legendary circus boss which was on at the London Palladium at the time, had been hired as stuntmen and they leapt off the real roof.

I am not entirely mad so I did not try to volunteer for that, but I did say to David that I thought that my wife, Carmen Silvera, waitress Yvette, played by Vicki Michelle, and I should all clamber on to the top of the real roof for close-ups.

As always, David listened carefully to what I suggested and said: 'You're not going.'

Eventually, after I had gone on at some length about cutting close-ups and my usual line that it would all look more real if . . . David did for once give in. He agreed that Carmen, Vicki and I would clamber on to the top of the real roof about twenty-five feet above ground level – but we were to keep still and hold tight. We completed the scene without mishap, but I have to admit it was pretty wobbly and there was a moment when I wondered whether David had not been right after all. I imagined us falling off, and my legs went to jelly at the thought of one of the women coming to grief, thanks to another of my bright stunt ideas.

Sometimes quite dangerous stunts are presented to you, and in the days before *'Allo 'Allo* I did a lot of commercials including one or two which involved some quite dodgy sequences. I don't think I ever said no.

I went to Spain to make an ad for Vodaphone, in which I was supposed to be a driving instructor whose learner driver had driven him off the end of a cliff. We are sitting in this Ford Escort suspended over nothing when the phone starts to ring, the idea being that even in the most inaccessible of places you can still use the telephone.

Well, I don't think either the lad who played the learner driver or I had realized that we would be hanging over a real cliff for some hours. But that is exactly what we did. There was a very strong, thick rope at the back of the car, attached to a large crane and that was our safety net, as it were. But the crane was on the far side of a road and the rope lay loose, with considerable slack, across the road. And as I sat in this vehicle playing with the Vodaphone it dawned on me that if the car did slip it would fall several feet off the cliff before the rope held, and we would be dangling there. Ouch.

Some years earlier I did a commercial for a margarine called Carousel which was shot in Leytonstone church. I played one of the bellringers. Now to learn to ring bells properly takes months, if not years, and I had two hours. Actually I did quite well, but I was warned that if the bell went over the top, in other words if it spun right around, then I would be taken off the ground and shoot up into the air. Now, it is not like that Morecambe and Wise thing when all those wonderful monks are left dangling on the end of their bell ropes. If it happens you get tossed into the air at a rate of knots and you can easily break your neck when you fall down. I did not realize how dangerous it could be, and went blindly into it as ever.

The inevitable happened. The bell went over the top and broke the wooden stay that kept it in place. I flew three feet into the air but then let go, dropped, and was fine. However, one of the girls who was actually a real bellringer passed out with the shock because a colleague of hers had actually been seriously injured in a similar incident some months before, and she could see history repeating itself.

It was a somewhat fated commercial. At another point in it I had to take a bite of a scone liberally spread with Carousel margarine and this man would come in and say: 'Was that you who played the wrong note, Mr Smith?' I would make a face, it would freeze frame and that was the end of the commercial. Unfortunately the poor chap got one of those mental blocks that can happen to almost any actor. He came in and said, 'Was that you that wrong Smith the note . . . oh, I'm terribly sorry.' He took thirty-seven takes to get it right. Can you believe it, that was thirty-seven bites of scone and margarine. I must confess I was spitting it out by the end.

Meanwhile the piece of wood I had broken had been replaced – another piece was made by hand and that took four hours – and off we went again. We did two more takes, and then it broke again and once more I nearly killed myself. Eventually it was decided to mock the whole thing up with someone manually pulling the bell rope up and down from a hidden place in the rafters.

The thought did occur to me that maybe we could have done that in the first place – but, in any case, I would probably have insisted on being allowed to have a go at proper bellringing. I know I would have been sorely tempted.

Recently I came curiously close to an actor famous for his involvement in some of the most spectacular stunts ever seen on screen. In the latest series of *'Allo 'Allo* one of René's many disguises requires him to dress up as a German captain. I was given a Nazi cap on hire from the theatrical costumiers, Berman and Nathan's, which I wore several times over a period of five days at different locations.

It is not unusual for items of clothing to be labelled with the name of big celebrities who have used them. On the fifth day I looked inside the hatband of my cap to discover that the last person to wear it had been Harrison Ford while making the third Indiana Jones picture. Now I would quite like Mr Ford's bank balance, but much as I enjoy stunts, I could not cope with having René swinging above a pit full of snakes. Being a coward of comfortable build René would have neither the figure nor the inclination for it.

Chapter Ten

A Kind of Loving

The most important love affair of my life happened when I was in my early twenties. It was with a merchant seaman. I suppose you always remember the first time you fall in love and the way it knocks you for six. Whatever else can be said, nothing like that has ever happened to me since. When I think about it now the memories are still vivid and a bit painful.

It is all the more difficult to put into words because I know there are those unable to accept that a homosexual relationship can be about love and tenderness and caring -- just like a heterosexual relationship. I do not know how you explain to somebody who finds physical contact between two people of the same sex abhorrent, that for the gay man, boy meets boy can be like boy meets girl. All I can do is tell the story the way it happened.

I was twenty-two. I had become very interested in sound recording through my work in hospital radio, and I used to subscribe to a tape recording magazine. There was what was called a Tapesponding section, and you used it to correspond with other enthusiasts by sending tapes to each other.

I started corresponding with this guy Peter who was a chief steward on a merchant ship, away at sea a lot of the time. To begin with we were just two people sharing an interest, but we did hit it off straightaway. We became too impatient with the tapes after a bit and started sending letters. Even these took two or three weeks to criss-cross. He was crazy and daft, and so was I, and the friendship was already happening before we even set eyes on each other.

Eventually we decided we would meet. He was on leave and had gone home to South London to be with his family, so I travelled down for the weekend and met his mum and his gran and various members of his family. I remember a load of us went dancing to a local hop and his aunt and I won a spot prize – chocolates and cigarettes. We had a lot of fun together. But we already knew we had something more in common. We had a relationship going. And we began to fall in love.

As far as both our families went, of course, we were, as the saying goes, just good friends. It was arranged that he would come up and visit me and my parents. I still lived with my mum and dad. He was going to Newcastle to see one of his shipmates, and at the end of the week he would come to Yorkshire. Everything was all very homely and ordinary. It was probably not at all the way most people imagine a gay romance to be.

He was due to arrive by train from Newcastle at about 6.30 on the Friday evening. My father used to get home from work early on Fridays and he was there in the house waiting, with his best tie on and a clean shirt. My mother was dressed in her smartest skirt and blouse. There was a cold supper laid out on the parlour table, with the decent china and cutlery that was only seen on special occasions. My mother was determined nobody was going to let themselves down, but she was a little bit apprehensive. Very Yorkshire, my mum. She didn't take kindly to strangers until she knew exactly who they were and what they were about. There were lots of nerves flying around that night. The three most important people in my life were about to meet and I was frightened to death. I wanted it to be perfect.

I was down at the station forty-five minutes too soon. Then the train was twenty minutes late. I thought the world was ending. After what seemed like forever he was there – exactly the same as before. The first thing he asked for was a flower shop. It was nearly seven o'clock by then but I knew one which I thought would still be open, and he bought this big bunch of flowers. He had a heavy bag with him, so we took a taxi the mile home. Peter got out of the cab, walked up the steps to the front door, gave my mother this huge bunch of flowers and said: 'Hallo, mum. These are for you.'

She melted. As indeed did I. I make no bones about it. She melted, and he was there, and that was it. He won her over, just like that, and she couldn't do enough for him. She thought he was the best thing since sliced bread. I remain totally biased because to me he was quite wonderful.

The relationship continued for about six months. Every time his ship sailed into Liverpool he would come across or I would visit him. Then the news arrived that his ship was going to New Zealand and he would be away for six months. We decided that for practical reasons we should stop seeing each other. It was him really, but I do believe he was living up to that old cliché of being cruel to be kind. The only practical alternative was for him to leave the merchant navy and stay ashore. There was no chance of me ever going into the merchant navy. I had just left the textile factory and started working in the office of David Brown Tractors in Meltham, and I had a family who relied on every penny I earned. Somehow at that age you do not always realize that you can change things. That you can make noises that will shape events in a different way, or even prevent things happening. Certainly I didn't realize it in those days. It is different now when you have twenty-two and twenty-three-year-olds earning forty grand a year and driving Porsches. We had been brought up to have a certain acceptance of the way things were, I suppose.

I was only earning a few hundred pounds a year, but it was a great deal of money in our house. My parents had kept me at school, bought the uniforms and the satchels and the shoes and all of that, and it had taken a lot of doing. They had made a lot of sacrifices. It seemed only right that I should start to put a bit back in.

One way and another, I never even considered the remote possibility of going to New Zealand. We decided, 'awfully sensibly', that our two worlds could not come together and we should end it all and go our own ways. It was unbearably sad at the time.

I was heartbroken. And I learned once and for all that you

cannot switch off emotions to order. I didn't eat. I didn't sleep. I was ratty and late for work. And so it was probably not surprising that one evening mum sat me down and asked me directly about my relationship with Peter. I suppose it must have been patently obvious, really.

But I should explain that it was only a few months before that I had accepted that I might be homosexual. I had always wanted a normal family life – in every way except when it comes to sex, that is the kind of man I still am. I am a pullover-and-slippers-by-the-fireside man, not a wild, nightclubbing partygoer.

As a boy in an all-male school, I experimented with homosexuality – dabbled is probably a better word – but so did practically everybody else. There weren't too many girls around, for a start. I never gave it a thought at the time. It didn't occur to me in any way that I was different from the other lads. I assumed I would have girlfriends and eventually marry one of them and have children. That is what people did.

I even got engaged once. I cannot remember whether there was actually a ring, but there was certainly an understanding. I met Alice soon after I started working in the mill sales office. She was a mender on the shop floor and I used to see her as I passed through the factory. We'd got chatting in the canteen and eventually went out together. I suppose I was about eighteen or nineteen, and for around two years we were accepted as boyfriend and girlfriend. We used to walk home from work with each other and go to the pictures. All the usual things. We actually went on holiday together once – but keep in mind this was nearly thirty years ago in working-class Yorkshire.

And our holiday was not perhaps quite all that it sounds. We were in a caravan at Flamborough with her parents. It had four berths, and she and her mothers were in one set of two bunks while me and her dad had the other set of two bunks. There was a sheet hung over a wire down the middle between us. Looking back at it, Alan Bennett would have had a field day. It was bit like *It Happened One Night*.

Now, although Alice and I had for some time been going steady, as the saying goes, we certainly hadn't been to bed together – that was considered a somewhat more momentous step to take than it is nowadays. You were brought up to behave yourself, or else. And there wasn't much opportunity, either. So I had never seen dear Alice early in the mornings. I had never even seen her without make-up and her hair done. As it happens that was all right – she looked fine – but what came as something of a shock was her early-morning bad temper. She had always seemed such a nice, happy person. I suppose I had put her on a bit of a pedestal. And suddenly here she was quite different from the way I thought I knew her, from the girl whose company I so enjoyed. I was almost certainly a touch grumpy myself at that hour of the morning, but that did not lessen my reaction. She was so stroppy with her folks for as much as an hour or two after she got out of bed that I have to admit it quite frightened me off.

Also by that time Alice was actually working in the office next to mine, and things got a bit heavy. She was just the other side of a glass panel, and there was a high desk where I used to check my order books and my shade patterns. I would find myself looking up and she'd be goo-goo-eyed at me. It was all right working in the same factory, but just the other side of a see-through wall was a bit much for both of us, I think. There was a lot of twinkling eyes and little waves going on. We were seeing each other too much at work as well as off duty, every day and most nights, and I am not sure that is the best way to keep a relationship going, not when you are that age anyway.

I think it was about the time I was planning to leave the mill that we started to drift apart, and I actually introduced her to the man she married. I was in the Technical College Drama Group by then and this chap was too. He happened to be with me when I was meeting her one night. He sort of slid into the picture and I sort of slid out, and that was that. It was all very gentle.

I got cold feet really. As I said, I certainly was not a committed homosexual then, and I was very fond of Alice. I liked her tremendously. But I knew something was wrong. I knew somehow that whatever I felt it was not really love, not really how it should be. And a little later when I met Peter I was proved right. He was quite definitely my first love and I had no doubt but that it was the real thing – it was all so powerful. I have quite genuinely never experienced anything remotely like it since. I suppose you don't.

And looking back, I think the truth may be that my mother thought more of young Alice than I did. She was certainly more upset than anybody when Alice and I broke it off. And I think her sadness and tears when she learned I was gay were to some extent the natural feelings of any mother for her son, but also to some extent because the scenario of grandchildren and dangling babies on her knee went straight out of the window.

Strangely enough, it didn't for me. And years later in Manchester, when I was in *Coronation Street*, I had another girlfriend for some time and she was a lovely girl. Janet and I had wonderful times together and the relationship was a true and genuine one. There was no question of my trying to camouflage my homosexuality by escorting beautiful young women to nightclubs and the like. I have never done that, and never would. But I know I did think – very naïvely, looking back – that I could get myself away from the gay side of my life and force myself to become heterosexual and marry and have children and all of that. I still had the vain hope that by presenting myself with an opportunity I could make myself fall into the accepted pattern.

But I suppose I was just kidding myself. The first love with Peter had hit me so hard there had been nothing since. No strong relationship with another guy. Accepting I was gay was still all a bit new. I did not fully understand what it meant. I thought you could control it, you could sublimate it, and it would go away. I deliberately tried to concentrate more firmly on the ladies, and on this lady in particular in Manchester. I tried to behave in the normal and straightforward way, taking her out to dinner, to the pictures. I thought that making the usual moves, fiddling with bra straps and all of that, was the way to what is most people's idea of normality.

I know now it could never have worked. And you put yourself in the position where you have to tell the person who matters most, in this case Janet, that the relationship is not progressing along the lines that you were hoping for. You have to back off.

Latterly I have longed for the kind of bond with another man that exists in a good marriage. In recent years Peter and I have been in touch again. Ironically, he has enjoyed a caring twenty-year-relationship with the same person. I have not been that fortunate. I live alone, and have in fact never lived with anyone. One of the problems with homosexuality is that there are no rules. And even the most liberal-minded heterosexuals do have the stereotype idea that gay people are usually promiscuous. Although that is a generalization, there is some truth in it. And so gays are seen as being hedonistic, uncaring, superficial. I hate superficiality in any relationship. I am not interested in a purely sexual relationship. For me, a love affair is about butterflies in the tummy and a vacuum where the brain used to be, about caring and worrying and wanting it to last, about loyalty and compassion and sharing the bad days as well as the good.

I want a situation where your partner will get up and make you a cup of coffee in the middle of a movie, or even the middle of the night. Where you take it in turns to get the breakfast or put the rubbish out. I want a fulfilling, complete relationship, and God willing it may one day happen. The trouble is, I get a lot of disappointments. I'm the sort of person who, if somebody is making the right moves and giving the right vibrations, I will go woosh, just like that, and jump in feet first, right over the top. I occasionally commit myself in a completely foolhardy way, too soon, too deep, and end up being very hurt.

I am terribly possessive, terribly envious and jealous of people in relationships. For a heterosexual man that is bad enough. For a homosexual man it is fraught with problems. I am not envious or jealous of my professional colleagues. But in my love life I want a one-to-one. I am prepared to do it, and I want any partner I have to be prepared to do it. To some extent that has been my downfall. I have tried sometimes to be more open-minded and to turn a blind eye. To say to myself that as long as I don't know what is going on then I don't care. But I kid myself. I never believe that.

I am also told that I make my partners jealous too. Not of somebody else, but of my work. I am quite single-minded about my work. I am told I can be intimidating, almost frightening, because of that. If pressed, I have to admit that nothing is more important to me than my work.

So I sit and dream of the perfect relationship with a partner who will put up with all my funny ways. I have given up any idea of ever having a proper family, or of having children. In the past I have thought of adopting, fostering, all of that. But, some fat chance. I adore children, and I hope nobody will misconstrue that because I am gay. It is in fact wickedly wrong to assume that homosexual men are quite likely to be paedophiles too. Statistically they are much less likely, as it happens. And it perhaps should be remembered when gay men are accused of being with someone under age that the age of consent is still twenty-one for homosexuals – and not sixteen as it is for girls.

I am just goofy about kids, like any man who would love to be a dad – and particularly like any man who would love to be a dad and for whatever reason can't. I specially like small babies when they can't talk but just look at you with those wide eyes and rubber faces. However, I just content myself with making a huge fuss of other people's babies. A family life for me can never be – but I have not given up hope of finding true and lasting love.

Chapter Eleven

Starstruck

My heroes are Jack Benny and Bob Hope. My favourite situation comedies are *Yes Prime Minister* and *Only Fools and Horses*. I suppose I have been starstruck ever since I was a little lad queueing up for a ticket to Wonderland in the cheapest seats at Huddersfield's Moldgreen Regal Cinema on Saturday afternoons.

I actually met Bob Hope when he was over here touring in 1984, and I immediately became an incoherent wreck because I was so over-awed. He was playing the last night of his tour in Preston and I had been making a film in Cornwall with Frank Finlay called *In the Secret State* and so had been unable to see any of the London shows. Hope was already well into his eighties and I thought I would probably never get another chance to see him, so I travelled to Preston.

Supporting him on the bill was a singing group called Stutz Bear Cats, and a mate of mine in Yorkshire knew one of the two girl singers. She had agreed that if we gave her a programme she would get the great man to sign it. We went to look for her after the show, and because it was the last night Bob Hope was wandering around backstage saying his goodbyes. My mate John suggested I go and stand beside him and he would take my photograph. 'Oh, I can't,' I cried, painfully shy as ever and in this case totally awestruck.

Somewhat impatiently, John strode purposefully across to Bob Hope and said: 'Excuse me, Mr Hope. This is Gorden Kaye, who has just made a terrifically funny TV series for the BBC, and I wonder if I could take his photograph with you.'

Bob Hope said 'Sure', was absolutely charming, and shook me firmly by the hand. The deed was done, except that John kept calling for me to look at the camera and I could not take my eyes off Bob Hope. All the shots were of me in profile staring at him, and jabbering away mindlessly, which I did for about two minutes. I could not believe I was shaking the hand of this God.

I remain showbiz mad and was from an early age. I do not know why – it certainly doesn't run in the family. The nearest I have to a showbusiness relative is my cousin Sheila, who is a really good singer. She never turned professional, but she has a smashing soprano voice and sings to a very high standard in amateur circles. She is in her fifties now, and I remember being taken to see her in a Gilbert and Sullivan operetta at our local church and being quite knocked out.

That, and the cinema and the Wild West show where I made my unfortunate début formed my childhood theatrical experience. As a fully paid up member of the Regal Cinema Saturday Club, every week I forked out sixpence or ninepence – the ninepennies were the posh ones at the back – and was usually treated to a formula diet of cartoons followed by a western, Roy Rogers, Johnny Mack Brown, Bill Boyd, Gabby Hays, et al.

I watched the films of all the screen idols of the time – Marilyn Monroe, Bing Crosby, Fred Astaire and Ginger Rogers, James Stewart, the great Bob Hope himself, Abbott and Costello, and Humphrey Bogart. Often after the main feature there would be a Laurel and Hardy short, a Pete Smith speciality, Joe McDoakes or the Bowery Boys. I loved them all. In between there was an interval for ice creams and lollies and sherbet fountains, and then anybody whose birthday it was would go up on stage and receive a Regal badge, while the rest of us would sing 'Happy Birthday'. Some kids had birthdays half a dozen times a year.

After these celebrations there would be The Serial – Naioka The Jungle Girl, Batman, Superman, Captain Marvel, or, of course, Flash Gordon. At the end of the show we lads would fasten the top button of our dark blue raincoats around our throats to simulate a cloak – all the Super-heroes had cloaks – and with arms outstretched in front of us we would 'fly' home.

Then the Huddersfield Grand Cinema switched almost entirely to a menu of science fiction and I was soon an expert on that. That was where I first saw *Invasion of the Bodysnatchers*. I was, of course, totally unaware of it being a political statement about the cold war between America and Russia. I just remember being particularly disturbed and distressed by the film – it's the one where beings from outer space arrive in pods and take over people's bodies. Images from that movie can still be very easily brought into my mind.

When I grew up I just became a grown-up fan. I greatly admire the acting talents of Anthony Hopkins and I turned to jelly the day when, carrying a tray laden with his lunch, he came across to my table at the BBC canteen, introduced himself and asked if he could join me. Once again I jabbered at him – I always do when I meet these people who are heroes to me. I think I must be an ageing groupie.

I saw Anthony Hopkins as Audrey the shepherdess and Derek Jacobi as Touchstone in an all-male production of *As You Like It* with which the National Theatre toured the country in the late sixties. I thought the whole thing was extraordinary – the idea was to try and produce the play the way it was done in Shakespeare's time, when men played all the roles. Seven years later the National announced they were about to revive the production – with the same director, Clifford Williams – and tour America with it. I immediately applied for a part – just a small part as William, Audrey's boyfriend. Then the casting director told me that Audrey had yet to be cast and suggested I have a go for that.

I did, and was given not only the part but also the chance to work with a man who was to become another of my heroes – Nigel Hawthorne from *Yes Prime Minister* – as Touchstone. And I had never been to America before.

The *As You Like It* tour was a terrific experience. We opened with a three week run at the Geary Theatre in San Francisco, and we had a ball. We were fêted morning, noon and night and it was difficult to get time to ourselves, but a group of us managed to drive across the Golden Gate Bridge and a few miles up the Pacific coast to a beach. I have never been a sun-worshipper. With a body like mine one has no wish to expose it to the eyes, not to say the ridicule, of the world – it might frighten the horses. So I sat in shorts and a T-shirt, reading and joking and drinking something exotic like Seven-Up, quite confident that I was perfectly well protected from the sun.

But when I got to the theatre that night I saw to my horror that the insides of both my legs were bright pink, while the outsides remained their usual blinding white colour. I appeared to be supported by two blocks of strawberry and vanilla ice cream.

I realized I had nothing in my make-up box that would convincingly disguise this condition and restore my pins to one acceptable colour, so I just powdered madly and got on with the show. As Audrey I was dressed in a white knee-length flapper dress – displaying quite an amount of the offending legs – and open-toed sandals. Gradually the colour returned to normal, but at the end of the second week we attended a reception and a local culture buff engaged me in conversation. After much effusive praise she remarked: 'I loved your Audrey' – or Oddrey as they kept calling it over there. 'The attention to detail was fantastic. I mean, here you are playing a shepherdess who would sit in the sun with her sheep all day, and you even made your legs up to show us what effect that would have.'

When we moved on to Los Angeles there was another reception, a first-night party in fact, which was a delight for a starstruck actor like me. Charlton Heston sent around greetings and champagne, Richard Thomas (John Boy Walton) stuck his head around the door and said 'Hi', and then Nigel Hawthorne took me to one side and said: 'Come with me, Zsa Zsa Gabor wants to meet you!'

I thought he was joking, but there she was in all her glory. 'Darlink, you were marvellous,' she gurgled. 'You remindet me of my fourth husband's ex-wife – ze bitch!'

I was already having something of a love affair from afar with America, and the *As You Like It* tour provided me with a memorable first visit. San Francisco is a stunningly beautiful city which seems to me to have everything. The whole of America is a

94

great showbusiness centre. California holds lots of magic for me. Hollywood remains the home of cinema. I disembarked from the tour's company bus right on Hollywood Boulevard, where the names of legendary showbusiness figures are imprinted in the pavement. It knocked me out. I stepped straight on to W. C. Fields, and I thought that wasn't bad. If it cannot be Bob Hope or Jack Benny, I will settle for W. C. Fields.

A less happy memory of Los Angeles is of Nigel Hawthorne trying to teach me to swim in the pool of the Hollywood Roosevelt Hotel. I have yet to learn to swim – and am quite ashamed of myself, as it happens. But lessons with Nigel were not particularly successful. He let me go under a couple of times, and after that I did not trust him. I am an absolute coward where water is concerned – horrified of falling in. The one time I am not at all keen on foolhardy stunts is when water is involved.

My grave reservations about Nigel Hawthorne as a swimming teacher did nothing, however, to alter my respect for him as an actor, and I also have great admiration for his *Yes Prime Minister* co-star Paul Eddington, with whom I appeared in a TV series called *Let There Be Love*. The secret of my number one hero, Jack Benny, as with all great comedians, is timing. And Paul Eddington is a master of timing. He has an extraordinary ability to start a sentence with one thought in his mind and finish it with another. You can see the cogs turning all the while.

The late Arthur Lowe was also a timing expert and could make an audience fall about without saying a word. I remember a scene in *Dad's Army* when, as Mr Mainwaring the bank manager and the Home Guard captain, he is in his office at the bank when he is told that Lady Ponsonby-Smythe or some such name is outside. He instructs Ian Lavender to show her in, and the lady sweeps by the pompous Mainwaring and greets John Le Mesurier, his assistant and humble NCO, with a kiss on both cheeks. John says: 'Oh, how delightful to see you again, your ladyship,' and she is just all over him.

The humour in that scene, of course, is when the camera cuts to a close-up of Arthur Lowe's face. He is appalled. He cannot believe this corrosion of his authority.

I have been lucky enough to have worked with a number of those whom I admire most. Marty Feldman was a genius who died tragically young, and in the mid-seventies I had a part in a series written by Johnny Speight called *A Speight of Marty*. It was a rather long and complex sketch in which a group of undertakers had to collect a coffin from the top of a block of flats. They could not get it round the corners so they had to knock on a door on each landing and back the coffin into the room.

On every level there was a guest star. Dandy Nichols, of Johnny Speight's big hit *Till Death Do Us Part*, played the mother of a bride holding a wedding reception in one of the flats. I was one of the undertakers and as we backed in with the coffin she told us: 'Put it over there with the rest of the presents.'

Spike Milligan was another guest star, portraying a trumpet-playing Pakistani bus conductor. For reasons which now completely escape me, Spike ended up taking this blessed coffin on his bus. We had a real London Bus which trundled around a secluded suburban housing estate not normally on a bus route. I imagine the people who lived in this quiet haven were a little bemused at the sight of a red bus careering along their tree-lined streets with a heavily disguised Spike Milligan standing on the rear platform blowing a trumpet.

Another favourite of mine was Alistair Sim. I played a Yorkshire Miner in his last film, which was about pit ponies in the early part of the century and was called *Escape from the Dark*. I was on location in Darlington and in the Yorkshire Dales for ten weeks, which was very nice for me as a Yorkshireman. But, as ever — certainly for those of us with only small parts — most of those ten weeks were spent waiting around. To while away the hours we amused ourselves by staging competitions to find an alternative name for the film. I suggested *Deep Shaft*, influenced no doubt by *Deep Throat* with Linda Lovelace, which was the big talking-point movie at the time. And I was thoroughly pleased with myself.

Peter Barkworth was also in *Escape from the Dark*, and I shall always remember a sequence which still makes me laugh whenever I think of it. Peter, playing the role of a new martinet mine manager, was paying a visit to the mine owner, played by Alistair Sim. The owner was interrupted in the midst of tangling with a new-fangled machine for cleaning carpets – to wit, a vacuum cleaner. The script called for Mr Sim to demonstrate to Mr Barkworth the efficiency of this wonder of modern domestic science, which was supposed to work properly for a while and then, after a few hiccups, blow a fuse and cover the actors with soot and dust. Technical difficulties caused this simple procedure to take nearly two days to film, and tempers were frayed.

We moved on to another scene where, following the collapse of a roof in the mine, trapping our comrades, a number of us were to attempt to rescue them by entering the mine through a disused shaft. We filmed this in a quarry, and the special effects boys had rigged up a lift cage that looked rickety but was in fact totally safe. It operated on a large piston powered by compressed air concealed beneath the lift – so although it appeared that we were being lowered on a cable slung over a very ancient pulley, we were in reality being gently lowered by the release of air under our lift.

None the less Peter Barkworth was apprehensive, having already experienced the difficulties with the vacuum cleaner. Along with him in the lift were myself, Jeremy Bulloch and Duncan Lamont, who played the foreman. At the back was a pit pony who took a delight in nipping people's bums and biting their coat buttons off. I should add, incidentally, that I was also carrying a canary in a cage!

As we came to the take where we would descend to rescue our mates, the camera pointed at us square-on over Alistair Sim's shoulder. A few words of the 'Keep a stiff upper lip, God be with you,' variety were exchanged. And as the cage started to move downwards, unseen by the camera but totally visible to all of us in the lift, Alistair Sim, with that benign countenance of his, made the sign of the cross. If you watch the movie you may catch a fleeting glimpse of Jeremy Bulloch and myself struggling to control a grin.

Also on that film Duncan Lamont was responsible for an amusing event, news of which spread very quickly through the entire company. On the first evening, before filming began, we had made our way to the location hotel in Darlington, and we were in the bar engrossed in a 'get-to-know-your-fellow-artists social session'.

Duncan, who had some marvellous stories about Hollywood to tell, was addressing a group of eight or nine of us standing by the bar, including myself, Derek Newark, Don Henderson (who went on to become Bulman), Maurice Colbourne (*Howard's Way*) and a few others. Duncan smoked roll-up cigarettes and talked with a ciggy dangling from his lips. As he spoke, his speech started to falter and slow down; then his eyelids began to droop, and very gently, standing there with the cigarette still dangling and all eyes still fixed upon him, he went to sleep. The peaceful drone of snoring could be heard to fill the bar, and for well over a minute the assembled actors all held their breath as one of their number stood slumbering before them. Then, with a slight jolt and a blink, he awoke and continued the story where he had left off, unaware of anything that had happened.

From that moment on, whenever a group of actors were together on *Escape from the Dark*, if anyone approached and started talking, the group would instantly close their eyes, put their heads on one side, and snore. We even dared to do this *en masse* one morning when the director, Charles Jarrott, came out to address us all about the scene we were going to shoot.

Apparently he looked a bit blank when it happened – I didn't see, I had my eyes closed – but a couple of days later, when he had to address us in a large group again, he stood on a camera box, began to say: 'Now what I want to tell you all . . .', then closed his eyes, put his head on one side and started to snore. He beat us to it, and drew a derisive cheer from the gang.

It was an interesting picture to make. As always, the location catering was something the actors really looked forward to, and on this film it was particularly good. A number of the principal actors were playing the part of coal miners and were therefore dressed in old clothes and tended to be covered in dust and muck – provided by the make-up department. So to differentiate between them and the supporting actors and the extras, the principals on this Walt Disney film all bore badges bearing famous Disney characters. We all ate the same food, but the badges allowed the leading actors to stand in a shorter queue and get back to work more quickly.

Mickey Mouse and Donald Duck were naturally on parade, and I remember that I was Pluto. One day, some weeks into filming, the caterers put Duck à l'Orange amongst the main course choices. This caused an outcry. We took the view that it would be like eating one of the family, made over-the-top remarks about the bad taste and lack of sensitivity of the chef, and all went for Beef Stroganoff instead. Only Peter Barkworth stoically chose the duck and was sent to Coventry for the rest of the day's filming.

That lovely actor Joe Gladwyn was in *Escape from the Dark*, and it was a privilege to work with him. He is best remembered, I suppose, for his wistful character voice-overs in those Hovis commercials, and for *Last of the Summer Wine*. He was a fine performer and a lovely man who had been in the business for years, and it was fitting that in the autumn of his days he should still be making people laugh in a TV series set in his beloved North Country. He still had the old variety performer's turn of phrase, and when we did the pilot for *'Allo 'Allo* in September 1982 he was recording an episode of *Summer Wine* in the next studio. I spotted him in the tea bar and went over for a word. After the usual pleasantries I said: 'Are you doing another *Summer Wine*, then, Joe?'

'Aye,' he replied. 'What are you up to?'

'We're doing a new pilot for David Croft about the French Resistance.'

'Any good?'

'Well I hope so, Joe. I think it's very funny.'

'Who's topping?' he said, meaning who had the leading role.

'Well, they're all good parts,' I said. 'But I suppose you could say I am.'

'You'll be all right,' he said, gazing steadily at me. He died not long afterwards, but I know he would have been pleased that his prediction had seemed to come true – and his straight, no-nonsense confidence was tremendous encouragement to me at the time.

I find it impossible now to think of myself as a star. In any case, the public can be relied upon to control soaring egos. After *'Allo*

'*Allo* had already been going for some years and I was beginning to accept recognition as a matter of course, I was standing at a supermarket checkout one day when the girl cashier said to me: 'Haven't I seen you on TV?'

'You might have,' I replied truthfully.

'I know,' she exclaimed. 'You were the man in the Zanussi commercial.'

I thought fleetingly of all the plays and bits and pieces of which I was secretly quite proud. And '*Allo* '*Allo* does attract its share of viewers. But I had appeared in a number of commercials in earlier days and the supermarket cashier was quite correct. I was indeed the man from the Zanussi commercial.

Chapter Twelve

Gorden with an E – Signs of a Misspelt Youth

I had been christened Gordon, spelt in the usual way, and I never intended to change that O to an E at the end of my name. That was a total accident which happened at the very beginning of my professional career.

My life was beginning to revolve more and more around the Bradford Amateur Theatre Group. The playwright Alan Ayckbourn was of considerable assistance during those early days. He had also described me as having a face like a squashed plastic balloon, which in professional terms is not quite as insulting as it sounds. He meant that, without the moustache, my face is so plain there is no distinctive feature between my hairline and my chin. My face is like a blank canvas that can be decorated with a wig or a beard or some kind of make-up to make me look quite different.

Anyway, I had been in a BBC radio play directed by Alan, and I had made my TV début playing a railway guard in a play produced by the BBC in Manchester. I was, after all, a local boy.

But what I was not, was a member of Equity. My name had already appeared in the *Radio Times* on a couple of occasions, and a number of people including Alan Ayckbourn had been pressing me to turn professional. So, unless I wanted to get myself blacklisted for all time, it was vital that I joined that hallowed actors' union.

I wrote to Equity and enclosed what I thought was my registration fee. They wrote back and said they needed another £1 10s

– it was long before the days of decimalization. And the envelope was addressed to Gorden Kaye.

I had never seen it spelt that way and thought it was quite ridiculous. But before I got round to writing back to Equity and putting them right I had a kidney stone problem, passed out and was rushed unconscious to the local hospital about two miles away. It was quite dramatic. The ambulance apparently roared through the town with its blue light flashing and siren wailing, and when I regained consciousness my father and half the family were standing anxiously by the bed, somewhat relieved to see me again.

At the head of the bed was a card bearing my name, which read Gorden Kaye. That was within six days of receiving the Equity letter. I took it to be an omen – or omon as I usually say when relating this tale. I decided to keep my name as Gorden. And so it was as Gorden with an E that – on the advice of Alan Ayckbourn, who pointed out that this was a new and fairly local theatre – I wrote to Robin Pemberton Billing, director of the Octagon Theatre, Bolton.

The letter was short and to the point.

> Dear Mr Pemberton Billing,
> I would like to be an actor in your theatre,
> Yours sincerely
> Gorden Kaye

The reply was in similar fashion.

Dear Mr Kaye,
Please prepare two pieces (not Shakespeare) and present yourself for audition on Thursday next at 10.30 a.m.
Yours sincerely
Robin Pemberton Billing

I had actually written so briefly merely because, having performed only as an amateur, I did not have a great deal to say. But I later learned that it was in fact the brevity of my letter which had attracted attention at the Octagon.

With great excitement I prepared a piece from *The Homecoming* by Harold Pinter – playing the lead role of Max. This had recently gone very well for me in amateur theatre at Bradford and called for a London accent. I also had ready a sequence from a play by James Saunders called *Next Time I'll Sing to You*, which demanded a straight Oxford English-type accent and which I thought was very funny.

When I arrived at the theatre I thought I had blown it. It transpired that, purely by coincidence, the Octagon was planning to stage *The Homecoming* in the next season – and there I was demonstrating my abilities in the lead role and I hadn't even been asked to join them yet. I had not had a clue, of course, but I was convinced everyone would think I was an arrogant little squit. And as I began to read Max my worst fears were indeed confirmed. I was aware of quite an atmosphere. Somehow or other I got through it and went on to my next offering.

Mr Pemberton Billing was sitting in a rocking chair on the stage in front of me and was accompanied by his assistant, Edward Clayton, who was also an actor and went on to appear in *Crossroads*. As I was performing, Mr Pemberton Billing was leaning back in his rocking chair and fiddling with his pipe, filling it with tobacco, puffing a bit, tapping and puffing some more, while he watched. After a bit he started to chuckle, sitting there rocking backward and forward, chuckling and puffing. I kept steaming on, and eventually he threw himself right back in the chair, roaring with laughter, and fell over with an almighty crash, taking the chair with him. From the floor he indicated with a wave that I should continue, and I did so. By the time I had finished, both he and Edward Clayton appeared to be enjoying themselves immensely.

I was invited to the office and the Octagon director asked me if I could sing. I was about to answer that I couldn't really, when Edward Clayton interrupted and said: 'You say yes to that one.'

I obediently concurred.

Mr Pemberton Billing said: 'As you will hear a great deal if you continue in this business, we will let you know.' I returned to Huddersfield feeling hopeful, I must admit, and wondering if I had done as well as I thought I had.

My excitement was dampened, however, because of my mother's serious illness. Sadly, she died the day after that audition which launched me on my professional career. She died on a Friday, was cremated the following Tuesday, and the day after that I received a letter offering me a six-month contract starting with the role of Pistchik in Chekhov's *The Cherry Orchard* at Bolton. It still upsets me that my mother did not even know I had got the job.

There were a few moments of uncertainty, because working at Bolton Rep would mean I would need to move away from home and leave my father alone right after my mother's death. But he insisted that I should go, and that he would cope, and I was sent packing.

I was, of course, delighted to accept the Octagon contract even though the weekly wage offered – £18, later rising to £20 – was little more than half of the £35 a week I was then earning, at the age of twenty-seven, in the textile industry. After sorting everything out with my father I put an advertisement for a flat in the Bolton evening newspaper and found myself a splendid two rooms above a butcher's shop. The rent was £4 a week and the butcher subsidized me with fresh meat – I was constantly being plied with delicious steaks and lamb chops and sausages, and have rarely eaten better.

The Bolton Octagon was a lovely modern theatre, and I spent a fascinating thirteen months there revelling in this new world I had entered. It was a happy company and we had a lot of laughs.

I remember doing a double bill of the Greek tragedy *Oedipus*, all very serious, and *Cyclops*, which was a comedy. We did it in fourteen tons of sand which was spread all over the stage to a depth of ten inches. I was in the chorus clutching a begging bowl, playing one of the diseased citizens who had to scrabble about in the sand. It was fairly boring, so to break the monotony we used to dig little holes in the sand and write each other messages and make sandcastles. We couldn't see a great deal because we were wrapped in bandages and it was most uncomfortable because the sand used to get under the bandages, so we had to do something to cheer ourselves up.

It was an actor called Ted Richards who played Oedipus himself who set us on the path to the greatest hilarity of all. He believed that you could say anything you wanted in front of an audience, you could come up with any absurd line you liked, and if it didn't sound right the audience simply would not hear it. That is not an entirely original thought in theatre. Indeed, years later in *'Allo 'Allo* we experienced something like it with Sam Kelly as little bespectacled Captain Geering, who could never be bothered to get his tongue around Heil Hitler at the same time as everybody else. It came out as 'Tler', and audiences rationalizing it heard it as 'Klop'. We actually had somebody write to *Points of View* to say that Klop was a real German word. However, I have never seen the principle executed quite as effectively as it was in that little theatre in Bolton one night twenty years ago.

Ted Richards was determined to prove his point. He said: 'I want somebody tonight on stage to say quite audibly the word "marmalade". And it must be clear and loud enough for the audience to hear it, not just the actors.'

Well, let's face it, the word 'marmalade' has no place in a Greek tragedy. But a young man called Tony Milner decided he would give it a go. He had to make a long, heavy speech all about Oedipus killing his father, and marrying his mother, and there would be rage and pestilence and laying waste of the land and drought and famine and desolation. As he finished the speech he cried with a great croak: 'Maaaaaaaaaaaaaaaaaaarmalade . . .'.

The whole cast just gripped themselves and fell about. The audience did not bat an eyelid. Quite naturally, as they heard the word 'marmalade', they convinced themselves that it must be something else – some strange Greek curse, perhaps.

We actors had considerable problems controlling our giggles. And in the comedy *Cyclops* which followed I used to play a very funny scene with Susan Littler, a lovely actress who sadly died long before her time. She was one of those satyrs with the woolly legs, half human and half beast, and I was a character called Sisyphus, right-hand man to the Cyclops, who had a big false head with one eye in the middle, wore huge boots and looked like a giant out of pantomime. We had a kind of cross-talk act for which we were allowed to ad-lib a bit and improvise, and that night we were on fine form and were going great guns, making the audience laugh and the cast as well.

Poor Susy Littler was crouched on this dreadful sand and she laughed so much, while at the same time battling to control her laughter, that when she got up from where she was sitting she left a damp patch behind her. We had to kick sand over it so that it didn't show.

For my first role at Bolton, as the farmer Pistchik in *The Cherry Orchard*, I had to age somewhat dramatically from my twenty-seven years to eighty. I had had my hair crew-cut for the occasion and I wore a false beard. Now the Octagon is a theatre in the round – the people in the front of the audience are practically on top of you. I remember these two local lads sitting in the first row and one said to the other in an accent you could cut with a knife: ''Ere, you can see where his beard joins.' And I thought to myself, 'He's right, you can.' So I managed without the beard after that. I think a lot of people do not realize – because of a staple diet of television, I suppose – that in live theatre the actors can hear the audience as well as the other way around.

I did actually appear in my audition Pinter play *The Homecoming* while I was at Bolton. The second act opens with a very long silent scene in which a family are sitting having tea, and the teacups are passed around and then the milk and then the sugar and so on, without a word being spoken. There are about eight people sitting on stage drinking this highly symbolic tea.

The sequence is supposed to build up to a moment of high drama. One particular night we were about halfway through all this – it actually lasted about seven minutes – when we heard a seat near the front go noisily 'Bdunk' as its occupant rose to her feet. Out of the corner of my eye I saw a lady walk to the back of the theatre – there are only nine rows – get to the door, turn around, and say to her friend: 'I'm going now, Enid. I'll see you at night school on Monday.' She was quite oblivious to the fact that the whole audience and the entire cast could hear her clearly. We got the giggles at that too.

I played a wide range of parts while at Bolton. I suppose I am lucky that I have always been a character actor. You have to accept that with a face like mine, you are never going to play Hamlet. But on the plus side, with the addition and subtraction of beards and wigs and moustaches, I have been able to take on a terrific variety of roles. I have performed in almost everything from pantomime to Pinter. And a character actor is always less likely to be out of work than a straight actor. Only slightly, though!

It was the very high-standard amateur theatre company at Bradford Playhouse which prepared me for joining Bolton Rep. I felt I was achieving more and more with the Technical College Drama Group, where I once even co-directed a rather ambitious production of *The Rivals* in modern dress. I applied to join the main hometown amateur drama group, the Huddersfield Thespians, and they rather snootily said they were not taking anybody on. The inference was that just because I had done this and that at the Technical College, I was not to think I was good enough for them.

A little crestfallen, I turned to nearby Bradford where the Playhouse put on a play for one week every month – for the other three weeks the theatre became the northern branch of the National Film Theatre. During my four years or so with them I played almost every kind of role in every kind of play. I remember I had a particular personal success as the waiter in George Bernard Shaw's *You Never Can Tell*. I even appeared at the Alhambra in the musical, *Kiss Me Kate*, in which I played the gangster who sang 'Brush Up Your Shakespeare', and I directed a production of *The Ghost Train* by the late Arnold Ridley from *Dad's Army*.

It was then that rather a nice thing happened. At a little reception after the first night of *You Never Can Tell* a couple of people approached me and said: 'Oh, Mr Kaye, we are from the Huddersfield Thespians. We gather you are a Huddersfield lad and wondered if you might consider joining the drama group in your home town.' I was able to tell them, with some satisfaction, that they had missed their chance and that I had no reason to leave Bradford where everyone had been so supportive. Small victories are sweet when you're young!

It was while I was at Bradford that a play in which I had the lead role won a festival competition judged by Alan Ayckbourn. Alan, then a radio producer with the BBC in Leeds, approached

me in the bar afterwards, said some rather nice things about my
performance, and asked if I would be interested if he happened to
have any little thing going in radio. I was delighted. A while later
he produced a play called *Definitely Not July* for the BBC, and I
was duly given a tiny part in it.

That put me on the BBC books, I suppose, and led to my first
TV appearance. I played a railway guard in a BBC series called
Champion House. A train had been hired at Bradford Station and
the heroes of the show played a small scene alongside, and then
boarded it – at which point I had my moment of glory when one
of them checked with me if this was the London express. I had
about two lines to say concerning the vagaries of British Rail, waved
my flag and we were away. We did a couple of takes, apparently
all went well, and I was sent home glowing with pride at having
completed without incident my television début – however lowly
it might be.

But later in the week I received a phone call from the BBC to
tell me that there had been an accident in their labs and the film
had been destroyed. They needed me to wave my flag all over
again. And this time they could not afford to hire a train. We
would have to use a real train – the London express from Bradford
– and therefore the scene must be shot at exactly a certain time.

The next stop, I recall, was Wakefield. I had to jump on the
train, wave my flag and blow my whistle while the departing
express was filmed, and then as soon as the director shouted 'Cut'
leap off while the train was moving. I managed this without injury,
but wondered how I would have fared had I arrived in Wakefield,
with no money, dressed in a BBC guard's costume.

During this time, when I was battling to get my acting career off
the ground up North, I used to travel down to London to the
theatre. A particular favourite was the Theatre Royal at Stratford
East, where Joan Littlewood was doing great things. They were
rebuilding at the time and the Theatre Royal stood amidst a
building site which looked more like a bomb site. I was there one
day and I spotted Joan Littlewood walking up and down in
the middle of all this mayhem, absent-mindedly kicking stones,
obviously deep in thought. I desperately wanted to talk to her, but

I knew of her reputation as an eccentric and rather erratic lady and I thought there was little point in just going up to her and introducing myself and saying I would like a word with her. I thought I should try to make an impression – to be direct and a little eccentric myself. So I strode up to her, and with a certain amount of aggression demanded: 'Why don't you give me a job?'

The great lady raised her eyes from the ground, gazed at me steadily, and replied: 'Because you're not fucking good enough.'

I thought: 'Touché!' And I just stood there laughing as she walked briskly away. I never did work for Joan Littlewood, although many years later I made a number of appearances at the Theatre Royal.

Kate Williams – who played my wife in the comedy drama series *Born and Bred* for Thames TV – was very involved with Stratford East and introduced me to the theatre. I did a number of plays and variety nights there and ultimately, in the mid-eighties, played Dame in the pantomime *Sleeping Beauty*. I was Sleeping Beauty's Scottish nanny, and the lilting Scottish accent helped my voice to hit those higher registers naturally.

That was the only time I have ever played Dame, and will probably remain so for some time. It meant a great deal of hard work, as I had to sing and dance and do all kinds of things I had little experience of. But it was a lovely and very successful panto. The theatre critic of the *Sunday Times*, Robert Hewison, compiled a review of pantomimes throughout the country and nominated me the best dame, which did wonders for my confidence. Perhaps even Joan Littlewood would have been proud of me.

Chapter Thirteen

My Wife and I

Carmen Silvera and I would still like to know who Princess Margaret thinks we were impersonating one night at the Adelphi Theatre. So if she reads this, perhaps she will give us a call and let us know.

Carmen and I are often asked to do charity spots as René and Edith, but on this occasion we were asked if we would do something different for a five-minute spot in a *Night of a Hundred Stars* charity show. So Carmen found this Noël Coward song called 'The Bronxville Darby and Joan', which is about an American couple who have been married a long time and, although everybody thinks they are the happiest couple in the world, the fact is that they hate each other like poison. It is a delightful, very amusing song, for which Carmen and I dressed ourselves as elderly Americans. Carmen had this grey swept-back wig and a black shawl, a long frock and little granny glasses. I also wore glasses and was clad in very baggy clothes with a cardigan, loafers and an old straw hat.

We performed our number, which went down very well, and afterwards the cast were lined up and presented to Her Royal Highness, who said some nice things to us. Then, as she left, she turned and made a remark which still puzzles us. 'You looked just like them,' she said.

Well, Carmen and I turned to each other and whispered: 'Just like who?' And we would still like to know, please, Ma'am.

As she is one of my closest friends as well as my screen wife, I spend a great deal of time with Carmen. Our *'Allo 'Allo* partnership seems to go from strength to strength, and it is enough for me to raise my eyes to heaven and proclaim 'You stupid woman', to get a laugh nowadays.

'I will come to your room at eleven o'clock,' says a gorgeous Resistance girl to René.

'I am sorry, I 'ave to share my room with a rather elderly member of staff,' replies the shameless café boss.

'The old boiler is playing up again,' he tells one of the waitresses on another occasion.

'I will go and 'it it with an 'ammer,' comes the reply.

'Isn't that a bit drastic? I will go and talk to her,' says René.

As Madame Artois, Edith is the butt of *'Allo 'Allo*'s most consistent and cruel jokes. Carmen allows herself to be the subject of these awful jokes, and that is an important aspect of the show.

'This is my wife,' says René, introducing Edith to a Resistance fighter.

'Will she talk?'

'Yes, constantly, but not about anything important.'

In the words of Victoria Wood, we are just like a real married couple – no sex and a lot of arguing. Perhaps that is what makes us funny to all those married people out there. And the dreadful singing voice remains a leading point of contention between us. Edith entertains the German customers in the Café René with her alleged singing voice, and her husband regards her as the Resistance's most effective secret weapon. When asked if Edith will sing, a typical René response is: 'Oh yes, but what 'ave the audience done to deserve such terrible retribution?'

Strangely enough, David Croft did originally plan to make Edith a real opera singer. It was Carmen herself who blocked the idea. She told David she felt she was just not a good enough singer. I know the thought of singing on television horrified Carmen. But David then had the idea of capitalizing on Carmen's self-confessed shortcomings and making Edith a bad singer.

And so it was that Edith the awful singer was born. Curiously Carmen, a highly accomplished actress with a proud theatre record as well as being known for her roles in previous TV series like *Compact* and *Dad's Army*, in which she first worked with David Croft, comes from a very musical family.

Carmen tells it this way: 'They all sing beautifully and play a variety of musical instruments, and when I was a little girl we used to have musical evenings. I was always struggling compared with the others, but I remember singing along doing my best when one of my aunts said to me: "Darling, do try to make your notes a little rounder."

'I didn't know what on earth she meant and so I pursed my lips into an "O" shape and made this appalling noise.

'Everybody laughed and I was dreadfully embarrassed. From then on I would occasionally be called upon to sing just to make people laugh. But my poor mother hated it when I did that, and generally I just did not want to sing in public any more.'

Carmen has, however, appeared in the opera *Carmen* with the Metropolitan Opera Company of New York when they did a season in Montreal. But she played a Spanish dancer – and did not have to sing a note.

She was a trained ballet dancer, and as such has a finely developed sense of rhythm. But she says: 'I do have great difficulty in carrying a tune. I am not exactly tone deaf – more tone dumb.'

She once appeared as the character Helen in a stage production of *A Taste of Honey*, and was supposed to become a pub singer and actually sing on stage. She said that was just impossible because she couldn't sing. At rehearsals, the director told her she was being ridiculous, everybody could sing, and told her to sing anything she liked for him to listen to.

Carmen told him she didn't know any songs. 'Sing "You Are My Sunshine",' he ordered her. 'Everybody knows that.'

She duly did so. She instructed everybody not to look, went into a corner, shut her eyes and sang 'You Are My Sunshine'. And she says: 'When I opened my eyes they were all rolling around on the floor laughing. The director insisted I should sing just like that on stage every night, and it always brought one of the biggest laughs of the evening.'

Carmen has even produced a deliberately badly sung record

called ''Allo 'Allo' with a screeching version of 'Under the Bridges of Paris' on the B side.

As René might say: 'It's surprising that something so round can make a sound so flat.'

Mind you, on New Year's Eve 1986 Carmen and I went live on the *Wogan* show and sang 'Ah Yes, I Remember It Well' from *Gigi*. It was a special edition of the programme, and we turned up for rehearsals at about 6 p.m. to find that we were scheduled to sing with a thirty-piece orchestra – not the piano we had expected – at 12.15 the following morning. By that time everybody else had done their bit and our nerve ends were totally frayed. We consoled ourselves with the belief that we would probably be appearing before an expectant audience of only a couple of dozen at that time of night. In fact I believe there were a few more than that tuned in, and it actually went surprisingly well.

Carmen and I have appeared on *Wogan* as a duo several times and I have often put something together. On the show where the whole *'Allo 'Allo* cast performed 'Chorus Line', I wrote the sketch seen first of all where René receives a letter and Edith asks him what it is. He replies: 'Oh, just another begging letter from that man Wogan. He wants us to go on his programme again.'

On the set of *'Allo 'Allo* Carmen is known to the rest of the cast as the Singing Defective. But in spite of all the jokes she puts up with on and off camera, we thoroughly enjoy each other's company and we have travelled to many places together. We have shared four memorable holidays – including a whistle-stop eighteen-day round-the-world trip in 1987. I particularly enjoyed showing Carmen San Francisco. It was her first visit and I had been several times before and loved it, and I got almost as much joy from showing it to her all over again as I had in seeing it for the first time myself.

We only had two and a half days, and we went up and down those cobbled streets, we went to Fisherman's Wharf and over to Alcatraz, and then up in the lift in the Hyatt Regency Hotel where the sides are open into this spectacular lobby – the whole height of the hotel – like the Hanging Gardens of Babylon. Lush green foliage everywhere. I told Carmen to close her eyes until we got to the top. I wanted her to experience the sensation of opening her eyes in the middle of this extraordinary interior garden.

We packed so much into such a short time, and one of the reasons we get on well on holiday is that we both like to make an early start in the mornings. Carmen is very good news on holiday because she is usually up and dressed and ready to go even sooner than I am.

I suppose because we have worked together for so long and spent so much time together, we have become very much like a married couple. And like any wife she is not afraid to draw some of my shortcomings to my attention. We are so close that I am sometimes inclined to forget about certain niceties of gentlemanly behaviour with Carmen.

Yes, perhaps I *could* hold the door open for her instead of barging through first, or help her with her vast piles of luggage when we are on holiday. And maybe I *should* think before I speak sometimes. One of my major faults is that I am over-pedantic about my work, and there are times when I am a bit of a bossy-boots and a real pain in the bum to work with. I am aware of this – most people *are* aware of their faults – but I do strive to be better-tempered. My bouts of irritation rarely last long, and inevitably the difficulties are resolved with humour (that good old standby again).

After so many years working in each other's pockets, as it were, it is surprising to a lot of people that Carmen and I are still speaking to each other. But we most certainly are. It was to Carmen that I immediately turned when I was troubled by revelations about my private life early in 1989. I love and respect all my *'Allo 'Allo* colleagues, especially Carmen – and when the day comes for René to hang up his apron, I shall miss them all terribly.

Carmen and I first met when we were working together on *Hobson's Choice* at the Theatre Royal, Haymarket, with Penelope Keith and Anthony Quayle. At the Haymarket, we did not play a single scene together and we had a lot of time off stage to kill. Carmen is a great games player and an organizer too – something of a games mistress really – and she frequently roped me in to play cards with her. She loves playing cards and board games and all things of that nature, but in particular she is a demon at Scrabble.

It is my belief that she once sat down in an out-of-work period and read the Oxford English Dictionary from cover to cover and memorized it. Carmen can get a thirty-three-point score with one letter added on to the end of the word you did not believe could possibly be made into anything else. And not only will she tell you that it is a word, but she will tell you exactly what it means – and if you have the temerity to go and check it up, you'll find she is right. So I refuse to play Scrabble with her on the grounds that it is monotonous to be soundly thrashed with such regularity.

But we do play cribbage. That was the game we used to play at the Haymarket, and we have played cribbage all over the world. When we went to New Zealand and Australia in 1987 we frequently played cribbage at 35,000 feet – very tall, some of these foreign hotels. That is the only obligatory joke for this chapter, you will be relieved to hear.

It was also in 1987 that I went on holiday to Majorca with some friends, and Carmen came along with us on the plane, as I had managed to find a particularly cheap package flight. She in fact was staying with friends of her own in Alcudia, which is in the north-east of the island, and my party were in a hotel in Magaluf, some fifty miles away. But one day we all met up for lunch. There were about twelve of us. I was at one end of the table with some new people I had not met before, and Carmen was right at the far end.

A few days later we were somewhat surprised to read in a London daily newspaper that this fairly raucous lunch party had become a candle-lit supper for two. It was reported as a romantic tryst between Carmen and me, and on our return both of us were visited by reporters from the *Sun* who wanted to know if we were having an affair – which, considering subsequent revelations concerning my sexuality, was quite ironic.

Our friendship, however, is a deep one. As long as you don't go near a Scrabble board with her and make sure she does not become separated from her belongings, Carmen is a great travelling companion. Once we stayed overnight in Los Angeles and Carmen left a suitcase on the carousel at LA Airport – which, as far as we know, is still going round. It contained lots of jewellery and personal things as well as clothes and was a great loss, but it has to be said that leaving things is something of a habit with Carmen.

She has a terrific sense of adventure. One year we went to Florida together and visited Disneyworld. We went for breakfast one morning to the Polynesian Resort Hotel, which is actually part of Disneyworld, and as we were sitting there tucking into the bacon and eggs there were all kinds of Disney characters wandering around to entertain the kids. A seven-foot-tall Goofy came up behind Carmen and put his hands on her shoulders just as she was lifting a huge glass of orange juice to her lips. She nearly jumped out of her skin, and the orange juice went up in the air and came down all over her. I have to admit that I just fell about laughing at the scene which followed.

An orange juice-drenched Carmen was trying very hard not to make too much of a fuss and, of course, the rule is that the person inside the Goofy costume is not allowed to speak. There was this great cartoon character looking thoroughly crestfallen, with chaos all around him.

As I said Carmen is a born adventurer. She is something of a big kid too, and insisted on going on virtually all the rides. Now I was happy to accompany her almost everywhere except on the Space Mountain, which is this enormous and very fast roller-coaster in the dark. I did not care for that idea at all and patiently waited for forty-five-minutes while Carmen queued up and went on this blessed ride, which so thrilled her that she wanted another go right away. I had to physically grab her hand and drag her off and almost slap her legs – she was like a child, quite desperate to go on the thing again. I just drew the line at another forty-five-minute wait.

On another occasion in Australia we were doing some promotional work and went up to Brisbane, where a fast city tour was arranged for us. We posed for pictures with koalas on the koala reserve, and Channel 7 TV took us for a high-speed river trip and gave us lunch on their boat, which was glorious. Then they took us up to their studio which was on the top of a mountain, and arranged for a helicopter ride over the city for us. I had never been in a helicopter before and was not particularly looking forward to it, but predictably enough Carmen was like an eager schoolgirl again. They put Carmen in the back with a girl from the studio and me in the front with the pilot, which was probably a mistake.

We came over the edge of the mountain and things started to wobble and I wanted no more of it. I am afraid I pressed the panic button and asked if we could return to base. I didn't like it at all. We had only been in the air for two or three minutes and Carmen was not having that. I disembarked and she clambered into the front seat and went off for her twenty-five-minute spin. She loved it, of course. I think she must have been Amelia Earhart in a previous life.

Chapter 14

Coronation Street – My Big Break

I had been a professional actor for only a year when I landed the part of Elsie Tanner's nephew in *Coronation Street*. The show was seen by 500 million people worldwide, and I remember sitting in the bath in my little terraced house thinking: 'Here's me, and I'm going to be in that. And I am going to be nervous as hell.'

I could not believe my good fortune. It was all thanks to Pat Phoenix, who played Elsie; to my mother's edict, which lived on long after her death, that you should always look smart when you go for an interview; and to a dumb jailer with big feet. My new job meant almost nine times the £20 a week salary I was picking up in rep. After all *The Street* was, and for that matter still is, the country's top-rated TV programme.

I was hired at the same time as Alan Browning, who was to become Pat's husband on and off screen. He took a great shine to her the moment they first met at a little gathering organized at Granada TV for three new members of cast including Alan and me. I actually joined *The Street* a couple of weeks before Alan, and I always remember him saying to me that day: 'Keep her warm for me, won't you?' It was a quite charming thing to say, looking back, particularly as he did indeed follow it through by courting and marrying Pat.

Pat more or less discovered me in television terms, and I owe her a lot. She saw me on stage in Bolton in a play by David Halliwell called *Little Malcolm*, which oddly enough is set in my home town of Huddersfield. Another coincidence was that Gavin Richards, who is Captain Bertorelli in *'Allo 'Allo* now, was also in that play. I was twenty-seven at the time and playing this nineteen-year-old wally with shoulder-length gingerish-blond hair, for which I wore a wig and contrived to look not unlike Jimmy Savile. It was a comedy role I enjoyed and had great fun with.

The Bolton Theatre was an extraordinary place. Robin Pemberton Billing used to suggest that we should all go to the bar after every show, and most people did. We had the magic of the theatre, all right, but subdued the mystique. Here was a provincial theatre in this Lancashire cotton town playing Chekhov, maybe, and all the locals would be encouraged to come to the coffee bar in the mornings, to have a look around, and to drink there in the evenings. 'It is your theatre,' he used to say. 'Don't dress up for it. Come as you are, and come and enjoy it and make use of it.'

And so all the cast went to the bar as usual after this evening performance, and there was Pat Phoenix and the friends she had with her. She looked at me, smiled a few times and eventually came over. She said: 'Am I right in thinking that you were the one heavily disguised with the wig?'

I confessed, and she said: 'You made me laugh so much, you really did. You reminded me of a neighbour of mine. Do let me know when you are doing something else.'

As you can imagine, I was thrilled to bits. I did in fact have rather a nice part coming along, so I thought, 'I'll follow up on that.' I dropped Pat a line and was disappointed when she wrote back to say that she was sorry, but she could not come because she was going on a tour with a play, but that she would come and see me again at a later date.

Subsequently she got in touch as promised and said she would like to come to see me in whatever I was doing at the moment. It so happened that I had the tiniest part in the world in this play called *The Shaughraun*, an Irish melodrama by a man called Dion Boucicault. I actually had *two* weeny walk-on roles, and in one of them I did not even have to speak. I was thoroughly mortified. And I considered it was just my final stroke of luck when Pat brought *Coronation Street* producer Harry Kershaw with her.

I made one minuscule appearance as the number two bad guy, and I also played the sergeant jailer in a British army prison in Ireland. There was a banging offstage and I had to come bumbling on wearing these big boots, red jacket, pith helmet, the full gear, and carrying a huge bunch of keys. In the middle of this empty set – the guardroom – was a revolving stage and I had to walk round the edge of it. Now as I got a third of the way around, the audience would start to titter. As I got two-thirds of the way round, they started to laugh and you could hear them muttering: 'He's not going to walk straight off, is he?' But that is exactly what I did, performance after performance, straight off and always to the accompaniment of a round of applause and roars of laughter.

It happened the very first night, when nobody was more surprised than me, and continued throughout the run of the play. I mean, if the audience had blinked in unison they might have missed me. Instead they obligingly split their sides. There must have been some kind of secret to it, but I never discovered what it was.

None the less I did not consider this fleeting appearance to be one of my greatest theatrical renderings, and I was more than slightly embarrassed to meet up with Miss Phoenix and Mr Kershaw afterwards, knowing they had come specially from Manchester to see me utter not a line. But Harry Kershaw said some nice things to me – and to my surprise, within a couple of days I was asked to go for an interview at Granada with a view to playing Elsie Tanner's nephew.

'No matter what you've got or how hard up you are, always keep something decent and make sure you look your best,' my mother used to say. So I duly dressed in my smartest clothes. I remember exactly what I wore – it was a pair of fawn slacks, perfectly creased, brown shoes, nicely polished, a cream shirt, crisply ironed, and a greenish brown tweed sports jacket with a colour co-ordinated brown tie. I looked like matching stationery.

I went nervously for my interview and was on tenterhooks for three days. Finally Granada telephoned me at the theatre, asked me if I was sitting down, and offered me an eight-month contract as Elsie Tanner's nephew at £175 a week. I was in fact standing up and I nearly fell over. It was like my birthday. And it seemed almost beyond belief to a working-class North Country lad who a year before had been working in a textile factory.

I remember a while later in the studio Harry Kershaw said to me: 'Have you ever wondered why you got this job?'

'Harry, I wonder why I get *any* job,' I replied.

'There are two reasons,' he said. 'Firstly, when you came for the interview you didn't look like an actor. All the people I was seeing had jeans on and foulard scarves and practically wore badges saying "I am an actor." You were smartly dressed, collar and tie, shining shoes, and you were different. Secondly, I've been watching theatre for over thirty years and I have never seen anybody walk from one side of the stage to another and get a round of applause. I thought I'd better have you.'

So the jailer did me proud, but I still puzzled about what the secret of it was. I could do with that kind of trick on a bad day when the laughs are slow to come.

Something uncanny happened, though, concerning that *Coronation Street* job. On the evening that I returned from the Granada interview to the theatre, one of the other actors in the company, a young man called Chris Emmet who has gone on to become a writer and an impersonator and to do things like *3-2-1* and *Sugar Babies*, was indulging in a bit of card reading. He was supposed to be quite good at it. We had just one dressing room for the men and one dressing room for the girls, and so this fortune telling was going on in the men's dressing room.

I got talked into doing the cards with him and he immediately said how good my future looked. He told me that money was going to be involved, something lucrative was about to come my way and it involved the figure eight – it could be eight hundred or eight thousand pounds, or it could be eight weeks or eight months. He was sure of one thing – that the figure eight featured strongly and was tied in with a great deal of money. Two days later I was offered that eight-month contract with *The Street*. I have never had my fortune told by playing cards since – I would be afraid that next time the wrong one would be turned over and I would finally run out of luck.

In 1970 my luck was up and running. Being on *Coronation*

Street with that terrific cast was just thrilling. Pat Phoenix was a wonderful, mad lady with a heart of gold. She was as dotty as a fruitcake in some respects. I don't mean mentally dotty – but she was so generous and over the top. She really was a star, and she behaved like a star in a manner that is rare in television. There was a blowsiness about her, and as she grew older she grew a little plumper, but it seemed to suit her. And she always remained a very beautiful lady with stunning hair who could glam herself up and leave any Hollywood superstar in the shadows. She had a presence, all right. She was magnificently equipped to lay it on for her fans, and she never let them down.

She gave me a piece of advice I have never forgotten. She said: 'Gorden, if you are running for a train and one of your fans asks you for an autograph and to sign it would mean that you miss the train – then miss the train. They have put you wherever it is that you are, and they are the ones that will keep you there, so try to remember it.' Now I am sure there will be people somewhere who will reckon that I have not always remembered that advice – but I do try to.

Pat's generosity was famous, and everything about her was larger than life. She had wonderful clothes and 150 pairs of shoes. I went with her to do a personal appearance once and I was in her home and I had forgotten my cigarette lighter. I remember I counted twenty-five table lighters in her living room. I reached out to use one and remarked how nice it was, and she immediately said: 'Have it, take it.'

No wonder Alan Browning was so taken with her. I know it went wrong between them and of course he had a drink problem, but when I knew them both it was all new and lovely. They were just getting to know each other and were very much in love. We had great fun together.

My girlfriend Janet and I used to go out with them as a foursome. We went to the theatre, we went to dinner, we went to Pat's house, full of Hollywood-style glitter and glitz, and we sat and talked long into the night. One night I remember we went to see *Who Killed Santa Claus*, starring Honor Blackman, at the Manchester Opera House, and when we came out one of Pat's most exotic fur

Pistchik in *The Cherry Orchard*, Bolton 1968. The lads were right — you can see where the beard joins!

An early Harold Wilson impression, Bolton 1968.

Above; Looking not unlike a seven-foot Dusty Springfield in *Imaginary Invalid,* Bolton 1969.

Right; Tetzel in *Luther*, Bolton 1969.

Below; With trotters on the shelf — making-up as Squealer in *Animal Farm*, 1985. What a ham! *(Eastern Daily Press)*

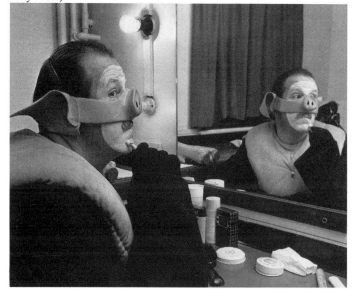

Escape from the Dark, Walt Disney Productions 1975, in my beloved Yorkshire.

Adolph never had legs as good as this! *Sleak,* 1977.

Mothers' Day, Royal Court Theatre, mid-seventies. *(John Haynes)*

Bernard Butler, Elsie's nephew in *Coronation Street*. Granada TV, 1969.

As the Rev. Grant in *Mansfield Park*. BBC TV, 1983.

Theatre Royal Stratford East, 1985. This is nothi[...] like a dame.

'Night of 100 stars', Adelphi Theatre, 1988.

At the 1988 Bafta Craft Awards. HRH The Prince Edward and Douglas Fairbanks Jr.

Michelle, Alphonse, René and Leclerc are interrupted by a passing radio-controlled goose, 1989.

Edith, Mimi and Leclerc protect René as he models Harrison Ford's hat! 1989. *(BBC copyright)*

Left; All at sea with Yvette and Judith Chalmers. Sealink Promotion, 1986.

Below; René with Edith van Gogh undertaking great danger, 1989. (© *Daily Mirror, photo by Bill Rowntree*)

The Paris launch of *'Allo 'Allo!*, Summer 1989.
(© Daily Mirror, photo by Bill Rowntree)

coats – a ranch mink I think it was – had been stolen from her car which had been smashed into. It was worth £3000, and in 1969 that was more than most people's houses cost up North.

We got into the car and decided to drive to the police station, but nobody could remember where it was. So we stopped at a bus stop and asked some man the way and naturally he spotted Pat instantly. 'Yes, I am Elsie Tanner,' she admitted. 'But please can you help us, we are trying to find the police station.' It was a lost cause. This poor man was so excited he could barely speak except to tell us over and over again that he could not wait to tell his wife. Eventually, I think, Pat managed to swap him an autograph for some directions and off we went. Meanwhile this £3000 coat was making its getaway.

But that was the affect Pat had on people. She pole-axed them. She knew Elsie Tanner backwards. There have been lots of attempts in film and TV to create a character like that – but Pat Phoenix's Elsie was alive, and people loved her for it.

She wasn't the only great one in *The Street* in those days, though, not by a long way. Doris Speed, who was Annie Walker, the Rovers Return landlady with delusions of grandeur, was one of my favourites. She used to do something very impressive which I wish I had the courage to emulate. Sometimes when a writer gives you a script it will say something like 'Annie Walker entering from kitchen', and then give a line of dialogue accompanied by instructions on how this should be delivered: 'huffily' or 'with venom' or 'haughtily'. Lovely Doris used to carry a roll of white sticky tape, and as soon as she was given her script she would stick a piece of tape over any such instructions. She may well have ended up delivering the line huffily or with venom or haughtily – but nobody was going to tell her how to do it. She would read the script and make up her own mind as to how she would play it.

Off screen, of course, she wasn't a bit like Annie. The opposite of grand, in fact. She lived in Chorlton, and she used to take the bus to the studio in Manchester every day. Once when I was staying in Chorlton, my car was in the garage and I decided to take the bus too. There was Doris up top, right at the front. I went and sat next to her and she was gloriously gossipy, wanting to swap bits of information about everybody else in the show.

Jean Alexander, the show's Hilda Ogden who only recently left, always used to travel in from her home by train. She and Bernard Youens, who played her screen husband Stan Ogden, used to play Scrabble all day long in a corner of the main rehearsal room at Granada when they were not needed. You could wander over and have a look at their board if you liked, but they would immediately stop the game and sit back in their chairs. They would talk to you for half an hour quite happily and didn't mind a bit, but they would not play until you had gone. What they did not want was anyone giving them any advice on their game – so they would just halt it until you went away again.

Violet Carson's most famous trademark, of course, was her Ena Sharples hairnet. But she was very fussy about her own hair, and every Wednesday would insist religiously on getting away early to have it done.

Margot Bryant was very different from mousey Minnie Caldwell, who used to sit in the snug of the Rovers, being walked all over by Ena. In real life she was a self-confident, witty lady who used to travel frequently to New York and stay in the city's famous writers' hotel, the Algonquin.

We really did have good fun making *The Street* in those days. Bill Roache – still there as Ken Barlow – used to do all sorts of wicked things to me because he knew I had a tendency to crack up. Always the giggler. He once had a squeaky toy under his arm which set me off right away.

People are inclined to take advantage of my giggling habit and I usually find, in almost everything I work on, there is one person I cannot look at. It is almost always a woman. In *'Allo 'Allo* it tends to be Carmen Silvera, which is unfortunate as we have so many scenes together. In *Born and Bred* it was Joan Sims. And in *The Street* it was most often Jean Alexander. When we played a scene together I just had to avert my eyes. And there was often plenty to giggle at, thanks to Bill Roache and all the other jokers.

Sandra Gough, who played Irma Ogden, was not the greatest learner of lines and she used to write them on beer mats in the pub. We used to move them around when she wasn't looking so that she would come out with the wrong line. Appalling behaviour.

The programme was extraordinarily professional, though. I have never quite worked out how they managed to maintain the very high standard of professionalism for two shows a week, year in and year out. No wonder *Crossroads* got so much criticism, trying to go out four times a week.

The Street is very much a bread-and-butter programme for Granada, and they could be forgiven for just knocking it off after thirty years. But it is not like that at all – it is produced with great loving care. I remember I had been on the show about four weeks when it went into colour. Now that meant different make-ups, different sets, new paint and outside construction because we had to have real bricks and wood, and all this was going on while trying to bring out two shows on a schedule that was tight enough without any fancy goings-on.

The management and the technicians did not believe it could be done, but a very clever man called Joe Boyer directed those two episodes, I remember, and *Coronation Street* did not miss a beat. One week it was in black and white and the next in colour, and you couldn't see the joins. That was quite an achievement.

I loved my time with *The Street* and would have been overjoyed if my contract had been extended, but it didn't happen. I think that could have been put down to my inexperience. I was perhaps a little over-eager and I did not leave the writers anything to develop my character with, to take him further. I do not think I had the experience to show them what I could do.

But I learned fast during those eight months. There were some fine people to learn from up there in Granada – even if none of them were able to help me solve the mystery of why that silent jailer brought the house down and thus helped me on my way to *Coronation Street*.

Chapter Fifteen

A Chapter of Accidents

It was a perfect evening as Nigel Hawthorne and I strode on to the stage of the 4500-seater Greek Theatre in Griffith Park, Los Angeles. This was the opening night at the second venue of the National Theatre's American tour of *As You Like It*. The back row was 150 yards away and being August it was very hot – but magical. We began in bright sunlight and ended up in a beautiful twilit atmosphere with fireflies zooming all around and wafts of honeysuckle perfume assaulting us.

A few days later the situation was a bit different. The stage manager announced over the backstage intercom: 'Attention, please. Try not to be affected by any audience movement on the right-hand side of the theatre – there is a skunk loose in the auditorium.' Luckily the visit was a friendly one and nobody suffered.

Later that week a stray dog came in and caused a great deal of merriment during a sequence featuring Nigel and me in which minstrels sang: 'It was a lover and his lass' and we danced a bossa nova. Everything was fine until the music started and our canine critic decided to accompany us with howls and yapping. The audience enjoyed it hugely and Nigel even tried to encourage the dog on stage – vainly I fear.

In the end, with brilliant Shakespearian expertise, Touchstone–Hawthorne addressed the dog: 'I prithee, sirrah, bear thyself more seemly in this illustrious company.' At which the dog barked, wagged its tail, and exited followed by two ushers and a tumultuous round of applause.

Sometimes a performance can be funnier when things go slightly wrong. Poor Richard Marner, who plays Colonel Von Strohn in *'Allo 'Allo*, was recently suffering from some kind of unpleasant rheumatic complaint which had quite badly affected one of his feet. In the best tradition of the theatre he adhered to the edict that the show must go on, and we went ahead with a matinée performance at the London Palladium. One foot swelled so badly that he could not get one of his boots off. He was unable to change his trousers and was forced to continue wearing his pale blue Goering ones, in a scene which called for his green German military jacket and the trousers that went with it.

So in order not to draw attention to the wrong trousers he sat at the café table with a car rug over his knees. The thought has to cross your mind as you cavort around the stage that this is rather bizarre. There, after six hundred shows, is Colonel Von Strohn sitting with a car rug over his knees for no good reason.

I actually think it is quite wrong for actors to be giggling at private jokes which the audience cannot share. But sometimes you cannot help it, and I am a bit of a culprit. Doorknobs coming off in your hand, people walking on at the wrong time, looking startled and then going off again, just sets me going. Of course often the audience shares it. At one of the last performances at the Palladium, I came out with a line that was totally wrong. It made sense but it wasn't the right line, and everybody on stage was struggling not to collapse. The audience knew exactly what was happening and loved it.

Arthur Bostrom, who plays Crabtree and is supposed to be speaking French terribly badly all the time, should be getting it 'wrong' on purpose, so when he gets it wrong by mistake that can be something of a pitfall. It is not very often he fluffs his lines, but we all do on occasions and when he does it can be particularly funny. He has to come out with carefully rehearsed deliberate wrong lines like: "I was pissing your coffee", and: "The RAF have bombed the hat". If he cocks it up the audience invariably twig at once and find it hilarious. I usually grin and say 'Easy for you to say', or something like that. There is a kind of double irony with him getting it wrong which is inclined to crease us actors up, and fortunately have the audience in fits as well.

In the TV show there was an episode when René was in prison and various people including the waitress Maria, played by Francesca Gonshaw, came to visit me in jail and brought me hacksaws with which to cut my way out. Maria had her hacksaw down her stocking top, naturally, and Francesca had to say the line: 'I will never let the firing squad shoot you.' And at that point in the script she got one of those blocks all actors dread. She said, 'I will never let the shooting squad fire you', which wasn't quite the same thing.

So we cut and tried again, and she said it wrong again. And it took poor Francesca nine takes. It was one of those awkward little lines we all know about that, in spite of yourself, you keep reversing. And when on the ninth take Francesca finally said: 'I'll never let the firing squad shoot you', there was a great cheer from the studio audience. They went up in the air, and there is this huge roar in that programme out of all proportion to the humour of the situation as seen by viewers at home.

At the end of making each series we usually put together a selection of goofs or out-takes, and we once decided to make a set piece out of the continuing saga of Francesca's beret. She was always losing it on location – it would just not stay on her head. So we had a goof day when Francesca would set off walking and her hat would fall off – again and again and again. They kept on cutting back to Francesca losing her non-stick beret.

Misadventure can often be funny and is indeed the basis of much situation comedy. I find that life is full of natural sitcom. Among the many off-screen stories of things going wrong for me is this one which, as is so often the case, is only funny in retrospect. It involves feet once more – although not quite so publicly as in poor Richard Marner's case.

In the early 1980s, I was on a grand motoring tour of Europe with a friend, when I managed to get my feet so badly sunburned I ended up in hospital. As I learnt to my cost during the American tour of *As You Like It*, I have fair skin and have to be careful in the sun. The trouble is, it is easy to forget about your feet. You know, you have on the hat and the dark glasses and the loose shirt with long sleeves and the 95 protection factor sun cream – and there, sticking out from beneath all this over-reaction, clad in sandals or worse still, quite naked in all their pale pink lack of splendour, are your feet, getting burned to a cinder.

On this occasion I was actually standing up to my ankles in the sea, the rest of me all creamed up and covered, looking into the afternoon sun while I smoked a cigarette. My feet, in the salt water which I suppose magnified the sun's rays, developed two luminous golf balls each. I had to be driven for much of the rest of the holiday, and travelled on the back seat with my red raw feet sticking mournfully up into the air.

But the scriptwriter in the sky had not finished with us and our misadventure was not over. An electrical fault caused the car to break down in the middle of a tunnel beneath an extremely large mountain. The hazard lights failed to work and I, of course, was quite unable to get out and walk. The day was saved by passing police who came to our rescue after spotting a red 'danger' triangle which we had put behind the car to protect us from the speeding traffic. What they did not know, fortunately, was that we had unwittingly stolen the triangle. We came across it on a deserted stretch of open road, thought somebody had forgotten it and popped it in the boot. Around the next corner were some major roadworks. We felt we could not really give them back their triangle, so we sheepishly kept on driving with our plunder safely stowed away.

I must have been going through an accident-prone period around that time because it was just a little while before, that I was involved in a motorway pile-up and then had two fingers crushed in the door of a police car. I had been taken to Barnsley Hospital with badly bruised ribs and was just about to leave to go home when the police arrived and asked me if I would go along with them to answer some questions. So I clambered into the front seat of the Ford Granada, gingerly lowering my battered body in and holding on to the door post with my left hand for some support. As I was sitting down a policeman got into the back of the car and slammed the back door shut on my hand, actually breaking two of the fingers. My language was somewhat colourful. The policeman was incredibly apologetic – but there I was with two broken fingers!

And as if that were not mishap enough, I then telephoned to some friends to come to the police station to pick me up – I did not realize until later that I had actually broken my fingers – and after waiting for ever for them to arrive, phoned again only to be told that they had been to the station once and the police said that I had left.

Cars have always been an important part of my life. I like motor cars, always did, and seem to be one of the few people left in the world who actually enjoys driving. In fact, during a period between *Coronation Street* and *'Allo 'Allo* when my acting career was going through a quiet patch, I worked for a local car auction in Huddersfield. We used to drive the cars around in front of the bidders at the auctions and then, if required, drive the cars to the purchasers' homes or businesses. As well as continual local trips to Leeds or Manchester we would quite often go on much longer journeys up to Scotland or down to London. And that job involved more than its share of accident and misadventure.

We would usually hitch back to base, clutching one of those red and white number plates that you see people holding by the roadside, announcing themselves as delivery drivers. But sometimes we would be fortunate enough to pick up an old car going for auction to take back. Some of these cars were in a right state, and I remember once driving back from Newcastle with four of us in some old banger, when the petrol pump packed up. One of the lads who was quite good with engines removed the windscreen washer tube, fitted it into the carburettor, then out under the bonnet and into the car through the quarter light window. We then happily drove along with the front passenger holding a plastic petrol can high up in the car, and feeding fuel straight to the carburettor through this improvised tube. Bizarre.

On another occasion we were given a car with a duff battery which we could not remove because it had actually melted into the engine compartment. I ended up driving all the way home from Holyhead with another battery between my legs, which was rigged up with some jump leads, again leading out through the window and in underneath the bonnet to the engine. At intervals a burst of sparks would fly up from between my legs, which was more than a little alarming.

The most spectacular incident occurred when a small convoy of us, accompanied by the company Land Rover, were driving three cars to Manchester, which was only twenty-five miles away. Predictably one of the cars broke down, and so a chain all of four feet long was produced from the Land Rover and this battered Triumph Herald was put under a none-too-safe tow. Meanwhile I had gone on ahead, but for some reason my car was only doing about ten miles to the gallon and kept running out of petrol – it was, of course, a point of honour never to deliver any of these splendid vehicles with more than half a pint of fuel left in the tank.

So I was parked by the side of the road just outside Manchester at the end of the Mancunian Way when this Land Rover, driven by one of our resident lunatics, came hurtling around the corner. The lad at the wheel of the Triumph Herald, rocketing along the road just four feet away from the Land Rover's rear bumper, was by this time in such a condition of terror that he had his foot hard on the brake of the Herald, stamping it into the ground as the two vehicles took the corner. So much friction was caused that the elderly Triumph was set on fire. It began to smoulder under the bonnet and beneath the front wheels.

We hopped about, trying to put out the fire – without much success – and one of the lads jumped over the barrier at the side of the road and knocked on a door asking for help. As luck would have it the door was opened by a Pakistani lady who understood not a word that he was saying. According to the legendary British custom of merely shouting louder in English at all uncomprehending foreigners, he bellowed: 'Fire, fire!'. She promptly offered him a box of matches.

Frantically, he pointed to our gently smouldering vehicle, glowing crimson in the evening light. Realization dawned. She ran into the house and returned with a plastic washing-up bowl full of soapy water and her husband, trailing after her in a bewildered and clearly half-washed state. The water was handed over the barrier and thrown over the engine. Meanwhile one of the lads had crawled under the car to try and disconnect some of the wires and he, of course, was duly drenched with a torrent of soapy water mixed with all kinds of oil and muck.

The burning lessened but did not cease. Somebody had the bright idea of looking in the back of the Land Rover to see if there was a blanket or any sacking which could be used to smother the fire. A piece of fabric was produced and tossed over the engine. The fire was eventually doused without major explosion, probably because I doubt there would have been more than a couple of tablespoons of petrol left in the tank by that stage in our journey. When the crisis was over, the piece of fabric which had helped smother the fire was found to be a donkey jacket belonging to the lad who had been half drowned by oily water.

Looking back on it, that was one of those totally true incidents which are much more absurd than any fiction you would dare create. It would indeed make great situation comedy – but I suspect it might be considered too far-fetched.

Chapter Sixteen

The Jobbing Actor

It was during a break in the filming of *Porridge* that one of the actors was telling stories about a thoroughly unpopular son-in-law. 'What a wanker,' he said. 'What a down-to-earth wanker.'

Somebody asked what this much maligned individual did for a living. 'I dunno,' came the grumpy reply. 'Something in the city.'

Ronnie Barker was razor sharp. 'Oh,' he said. 'A merchant wanker.' It was a lovely line and came out so fast and perfectly timed, it was as if it had been carefully written and rehearsed. Ronnie has a mind like a rat trap.

On another occasion we were playing cards on set and about five of the cards turned out to be missing, so we asked the fourth assistant who was looking after us, to pop across the road and get us a new pack. Then someone said: 'No, we don't need a full set, just ask for a five of clubs and a jack of hearts and so on. . . .'

Everybody laughed, but Ronnie went straight into a sketch. Without any kind of script, he stood up, and went into this scenario with a shopkeeper that was funnier than a lot of sitcoms I have seen. 'Good morning, I would like some playing cards. I would like a six of diamonds, two queens of spades, two tens of . . . what's that? Yes, that's right. I cheat.'

He was hilarious. If there is one professional I would like to be, it is Ronnie Barker. I think he is the best. I remain more than a little in awe of him and was quite impressed to be working with him and Richard Beckinsale, who died so tragically young, on the feature film of *Porridge*. The TV series was already a huge success. We were shooting at Chelmsford Jail – which, rather conveniently, had been temporarily closed because of a fire. So nowadays if anyone mentions Chelmsford, I always say: 'Ah yes, Chelmsford. I was in prison in Chelmsford.'

Now filming only seems like a glamorous way of making a living to those who have never experienced it. It always involves more waiting around than anything else, frequently in thoroughly unpleasant conditions, and so these lighter moments of fooling around play quite an important part in keeping the brain alive. Ronnie loved to make people laugh on set and to be made to laugh himself.

Porridge was shot in February, naturally, and it was freezing cold, naturally. We had to be on set for make-up at 6.30 in the morning, and the prison hospital was being used as a make-up room. It resembled a more than usually efficient refrigerator, and the actors were the slabs of chilled meat. I remember one morning we were all sitting around in our thermal underwear slowly freezing and Ronnie was in the chair having his hair coloured red for his part of the likeable con, Fletcher – his hair is naturally silver, of course.

I was standing behind him and I did the old John Wayne impression. John Wayne pulls his gun out and drawls: 'OK. Put your hands up you bum.' The standard somewhat risqué reply is: 'Put your hands up your own bum.'

Well, Ronnie started to laugh and he couldn't stop. Hysteria brought on by the bitter cold, probably. And all through the day he would catch my eye, adopt the John Wayne stance and mime pulling a gun out of his pocket.

I had a small part, but a very nice part, in the film, and I worked on it for quite a while. Peter Vaughan, who played the Mr Big prisoner, was trying to arrange an escape and forced Fletcher to organize a football match with a celebrity soccer eleven brought in to play the prison team. I was the bus driver, and the idea was that the escaping prisoner should be swapped for me. I was attacked, stripped to my vest and underpants, and tied to the cistern in the lavatory, so I spent most of my time during this icy February shivering in the loo.

I knew Richard Beckinsale very well before the film. In fact we shared a cottage once in Leeds. We met while I was acting in a production of *Toad of Toad Hall*. He was already living with Judy Loe, whom he later married, in London, but he came up North to play *Romeo and Juliet*. It was a repertoire system so he would go back to London when he could, but on and off we shared this pretty little cottage just outside of Leeds for three months. We had a cat that came with the house, a big ginger cat called Friday because, according to the people who owned the house, it had arrived on Friday. Friday used to leave us little presents in the bath, and would never leave them at the plug hole end – always the other end. And it always seemed to be my job to clean them up, somehow. But Judy used to come up occasionally and spend the weekend with us and sort us out. She used to cook us lovely moussakas and spoil us a bit.

It was a terrible shock for her and for everybody when Richard died so suddenly – just two weeks after we had finished filming *Porridge*. I remember I was at home in bed nursing a bad cold when I heard the news on the radio. I could not believe it. He was only thirty-four and had always seemed very fit. He liked to play hard but he worked very hard too. He liked a drink and he seemed to have the ability to roister with the best of them, and two hours later be on set bright as a button, fresh as a daisy, while everyone else had headaches and was still falling over.

This all happened in 1979. I was out of *Coronation Street* and making my living as a jobbing actor. I went through a lean patch at first and survived largely through a certain amount of kiddology. If I got any acting work at all in any one month I would say to myself that was my January job, or my February job, and so on. And after three months or so I would kid myself I was doing OK because I had been in work for three months. I may have spent only twenty weeks working in a year and the other thirty or so signing on, but that was the way I looked at it and it got me through. Also, thanks to my working-class background I knew how to pull in my horns. My mother always told me you should cut your coat to suit your cloth.

Anyway, it was during that twelve-year period of my life between

The Street and *'Allo 'Allo* that I worked with some great people. Leonard Rossiter, of course, was best known for his TV situation comedies, the Reginald Perrin series and *Rising Damp*. But he was possibly the finest technical comedy actor this country has ever produced, and his technique on stage and in films was also brilliant. I have seen him at the Haymarket Theatre stand as far downstage and as far right as you can get, which is just where you do not want to be to command an audience. You want to be as far upstage and as near centre as you can. But I have seen him from this remote corner of the stage lift an eyebrow and lift an audience out of their seats with laughter.

I worked with him once in a tiny little film called *The Waterloo Bridge Handicap*, in which commuters arrived at Waterloo Station in the same carriage, on the same train every morning and went through the barrier on their way to work, walking over Waterloo Bridge. The idea was that there was a kind of race going on and they were all competitors with names and form just like horses. There was Chubby Chap, which was me, and Blue Suit, and Henna Rinse. You weren't allowed to run, and if somebody approached you with a survey or the pedestrian lights were against you, you had to stop.

Well, one day we had to stop the whole thing because it was tipping down with rain and we stood under Waterloo Bridge by the National Film Theatre for some hours, hoping for an improvement. It would have been pretty boring and miserable but for Leonard, who regaled us all with wonderful stories and little sketches.

He told us about an Oscar Wilde play he did in Worthing or Dorking or somewhere, for which he had to wear a dress suit which had been hired from a small theatrical costumiers. They are inclined to be somewhat tatty and frayed at the edges, well worn and smelling of mothballs. Leonard was sitting centre stage on a velvet sofa in this elegant drawing room in the middle of the play, when his lady wife had to say to him dramatically: 'Oh, Charles. What has gone wrong with our marriage?' At that moment a moth flew out of his trouser flies. And there was the answer. That was what was wrong with the marriage – moths in the crutch.

Leonard also used to perform a lovely set piece in which he would say: 'Have you ever walked past a tailor's shop window and wondered how the models got into those positions?' He would then proceed to act out all the absurd, unlifelike poses you see tailor's dummies in. Bottom out, chest in, fingers at impossible angles all over the place. A great comic talent and sadly missed.

In the late seventies, I also worked with Leonard's wife Gillian Raine in the Thames TV comedy drama series *Born and Bred*, written by Douglas Livingstone, about two large South London families, all inter-related and inter-married. I had been spotted for the role of downtrodden husband, Ray Benge, by a casting lady who saw me in a very strange play at London's Royal Court, called *Sleek*. It was a snuff rock musical comedy which took punk a stage further. The idea was that the lead singer would kill himself at the end of every show and they would have to have a new one every night. It was funnier than it sounded and very successful, running for four years on and off at the Royal Court and in America, Holland and Germany.

Somehow this led the producers of *Born and Bred*, in their wisdom, to think I was just right to play Ray Benge. Their only worry was that being a Yorkshireman my London accent would not be good enough. Eventually they decided I would do, and in any case I had my screen wife to keep me on track. Kate Williams, who is a Londoner, used to whisper, 'Ee by gum, ee by gum' at me out of the corner of her mouth – which meant, of course, that she reckoned I was getting a bit Yorkshire.

Joan Sims, big James Grout (a real favourite of mine who was in my *This Is Your Life*) and Max Wall were also in that show – and we made two series. Jimmy Grout, I fear, is another one who makes me corpse. We just could not stop giggling through one sequence of *Born and Bred*, and in the end the director came down from his box and really tore us off a strip. I mean, he wagged his finger at us and pointed out that there were several dozen technicians and other people waiting to get this done. We were just behaving like children and we were to stop giggling and get on with it. I am ashamed to say that as soon as he went back upstairs we started giggling again. We were out of control. Eventually, and in exasperation, he called an early lunch.

It was a real privilege to work with a legendary figure like Max Wall, who was then already in his mid-seventies. We were sitting in a pub during a break in rehearsals one day and Max was having his usual pint of Guinness – he loves his Guinness – and captivating us with stories of the old days. Max Wall has been around a long, long time. He had been a clown with a superb mastery of the art of mime, and he even worked with Grock in Paris. I could listen to his tales for ever.

Now Max had not been seen on TV for a bit at that time – and to many people television is showbusiness. If you are not on the box then you are not working. And so this little man came up and hovered by our table, and finally said: 'Mr Wall, it's nice to see you making a come-back.'

Max gave him that unique bleak look and said very simply in that totally inimitable voice: 'I haven't been anywhere.'

It was also while making *Born and Bred* that I witnessed a lovely scene with another great clown, Tommy Cooper. We were in the waitress service restaurant at Thames TV in Teddington, where there are about twelve or thirteen tables. Tommy and some colleagues were sitting not far from my table. He had ordered wine, and when the waitress brought the bottle she poured a little into a glass for Tommy to taste.

He picked it up, sipped, clutched his throat, threw himself backwards on his chair and fell with a crash on to the floor. Everybody gasped. The waitress looked as if she was going to fall over herself. Before anyone had time to do anything, Tommy was on his feet. He set his chair upright, sat down on it and said: 'Thank you very much, that will be fine.'

It brought the house down. For anybody to go through the whole of that in their lunch break in a TV studio restaurant is just extraordinary.

The great ones never miss an opportunity to make people laugh. Les Dawson is one of the most quick-witted, and there is no subject he will not find a laugh in. I used to work on his *Sez Les* series with him and Roy Barraclough, who is now Rovers Return landlord

Alec Gilroy in *Coronation Street*, and one day we were talking through ideas for quick one-liner sketches and trying to remember when certain things had last been done.

Suddenly Les said: 'When did we last do the Prisoner of Zenda thing? You know, hanging from the ceiling and all of that.' Nobody was quite sure which series, but finally there was one man who could remember exactly and in some detail.

'Just call me Mr Mothballs,' he quipped.

There was not a pause. 'Didn't he die of camphor?' asked Les.

Les Dawson is one of the most relaxed performers I have ever seen – at least if he isn't, he puts on the best act I have ever seen. Maybe what he does is switch off and simply not think about what is happening until he is before the camera, but it is very impressive whatever the secret. During the making of *Sez Les*, while everyone else was on tenterhooks right before the show Les would be in the bar having a gentle gin and tonic. There he would stay until he was called to go on, and then he would just walk straight on to the floor and tear them apart. He would always have the audience eating out of his hand. Les is so together.

I do get nervous. I suffer from butterflies with hobnailed boots on. But, to be honest, I believe that when I stop suffering from nerves, I won't be any good any more. All of us are different.

Les Dawson was very kind to me once, probably without knowing it, when I was making my first guest appearance in *Are You Being Served?* with John Inman and Molly Sugden. It was already a very well-established series and I was an interloper. Now everyone was terribly nice to me – it was a David Croft show, of course, and all his productions are inclined to be happy – but nobody knew who on earth I was in those days, so naturally I was a bit of an outsider. And Les established a pedigree for me.

We were in the canteen – yes, I know, again – and I was queuing up to get something to eat, when Les, who was right across the room, left his table and came over and greeted me, clapped me on the back and said how nice it was to see me, and we should have lunch and all that. I knew everybody in the room was looking to see who it was that Les Dawson had gone out of his way to speak to. I could no longer possibly be an outsider after that.

Les and Max Wall and Frankie Howerd and Tommy Cooper are all that particular kind of British character comedian who are, for want of a better word, and not meant unkindly, grotesque. You get Les, five feet high and five feet wide, and you put him in a frock doing Cissy and Ada and it is instantly funny. American comics are all smoothly handsome in flash blue suits. Our best ones are like Tommy Cooper, a walking disaster. And when Frankie Howerd says: 'This wonderful bird came up to me – it was obvious she was fancying me rotten,' that is funny because it is so totally unlikely.

I know I am of that breed of comedian myself, and René is certainly that kind of character. One of the standing jokes about this not very attractive overweight Frenchman is that all these women are fighting over him – and you know that cannot be for real. It would not be funny if he were a handsome young Adonis.

One man I worked with in the seventies and whom I was quite terrified of was Warren Mitchell. I had a small part in *Till Death Do Us Part*, in which I was supposed to be a television licence officer calling around to ask Alf Garnett why he did not have a licence. Anyone who remembers the programmes or saw the recent repeats can imagine the kind of reception I got, even if they cannot remember that particular episode.

I had been warned in advance by those with reason to know that Warren Mitchell was a perfectionist and could be very tough, and I was more than a little apprehensive working with him and this very slick team of situation comedy actors, Dandy Nichols, Una Stubbs and Tony Booth. In fact I was just feeding Alf Garnett's anger. I had one line and then he had three more paragraphs, so I didn't really need to worry.

A guest appearance I thoroughly enjoyed, was playing a Yorkshire pig farmer in the James Herriot vet series *All Creatures Great and Small*, with Christopher Timothy, Robert Hardy and Peter Davison. Of course there was an element of going home about it – there I was in the heart of the Yorkshire Dales, one of my favourite places in all the world – and also it was a smashing little part. I was this big softy of a farmer who was going to have to sacrifice his pet pig called Wilfred to feed his family, and he was very distressed about it.

I was duly introduced to this large pig who was to play Wilfred. I watched while its owner and a couple of handlers drove it out of its trailer and into a little pen, and I was amazed at how enormous it was. I had to deal with it at close quarters and I didn't much like the look of Wilfred. So I said to this very laconic farmer: 'Has it had its breakfast?'

'Aye,' he replied expressionlessly. 'He's 'ad a bit of food.'

'Will it bite?' I asked.

'It might do,' he said, without much interest.

I was not too happy and did my best to keep away from the dangerous end. Actually Wilfred behaved himself quite nicely, and it is possible his owner was merely relishing my discomfort. But when Christopher Timothy brought a piglet he claimed was the son of Wilfred on to my *This Is Your Life* programme, there was slightly more of an in joke there than viewers would have realized.

Working with David Croft marked the beginning of new and wonderful things for me, of course, and I made two appearances on *Are You Being Served?* at the height of its success, which I was overjoyed about even though they were just small parts. First I played a Greek whose brother had proposed marriage to Mrs Slocombe, Molly Sugden. I had to break the news that the scallywag already had a wife. Then I played a man who goes into the store to buy a plastic raincoat. He stands in front of the mirror, puts his hands in his pockets, opens the coat very wide and then closes it again quickly, like a flasher. Mr Humphries, John Inman, is quite amazed by this exhibition – then it is explained that my character is a paparazzi photographer, and the raincoat allows him to jump out in front of well-known personalities and flash his camera.

I read the script and turned up at the BBC's North Acton rehearsal rooms, the Acton Hilton as it is known, where I suggested to David Croft that I should play the paparazzi character as a Scotsman in a kilt. David and I already had the kind of relationship where he would allow me to make suggestions, but on this occasion he looked at me aghast and asked: 'In God's name why?'

I said: 'Well, I just had this idea that you could put the camera in the sporran, and the sporran would pop up and flash and go back down again, and that would give us another laugh.'

'I'll think about it,' said David. And by the end of the week I was a Scotsman in all the gear with a dirk down the top of my socks and a tam o'shanter and a very strong Scottish accent, which I do quite easily because I am partly Scots.

David let me put in a couple of lines as well. I said to John Inman: 'Some of my friends call me Candid Cameron.' And he replied: 'If you wear this mac they'll be able to call you Gabardine Angus.' So I had a laugh, and I had thought of a line with a laugh that topped it – which made it all right.

Subsequently David hired me to be in a series called *Come Back Mrs Noah* which he had written for Ian Lavender and Molly Sugden. It was set in the year 2050 and was about Britain's first space station which Molly, as Housewife of the Year, was invited to tour. Basically she pushed the wrong button and bingo – the thing is launched and The Housewife of the Year becomes a spacewoman.

My role was as a ground-based news reporter – like somebody from *Newsnight* – and each week I would head up the programme with a news report. David used to let me write some of my own material for that – I would often be given a script which would start with a blank page which just said four, or however many, jokes from Gorden. It was all little news items about things that were relevant in 1978 or 1979 moved on seventy years or so to the year 2050. There was 'Prince Charles, 101, is still having an affectionate relationship with Lady Jane Wellesley', and a story about the winner of the Eurovision Song Contest being Cliff Ricardo.

I remember I used to write quite naughty jokes for the dress rehearsal that we could not put on the air, but once David wrote a line himself which he later became worried about but could see no way of cutting. I had to read an item about trouble at the British Leyland Robot Factory where there was an industrial dispute caused by a strike in the tool works. Considering what we get away with in *'Allo 'Allo* nowadays it was all very demure stuff, but that was 1978 and eleven years is a long time in television.

Sadly, *Come Back Mrs Noah* is one of the very few David Croft sitcoms that only ran the one series. It was a shame because it was actually very good, I think, but it didn't do too well in the ratings because it was scheduled rather unfortunately. It went out right opposite Kenny Everett's first venture into television, which was new and big and exciting. David has said since that he regrets he did not nurse the show back to life and push for it more, but it was not to be.

I had first worked for David a year before *Mrs Noah*, in 1977, on *It Ain't Half Hot Mum*. I had never met him, but his PA, Gordon Elsbury, who went on to direct *Top of the Pops*, *The Tube* and Jonathan Ross's *Last Resort*, and to produce Jonathan King in *Entertainment USA*, spotted me in *Sleek* – that snuff rock musical again. That has a lot to answer for. He thought I would be right for the role of a soldier in the audience at a concert party who kept shouting out the tag lines to the comedian's jokes and spoiling the gags.

The show was shot on location down in Aldershot; with apologies to those who still think it was all out in Burma, it was actually filmed in our very own British army tank traps, an hour's train ride out of London Waterloo. I was summoned on the second day of location filming, and all the signs that had been up on the first day saying: 'Units this way', and so on, had been taken down. The taxi driver who met me at the station didn't have a clue where to go and neither did I. We drove around military-looking areas for a long, long time and eventually met up with a lady whose rather small car was laden with a rather large monkey and a parrot in a cage. She was looking for the location, too, and unfortunately could not find it either.

Then to our relief, we spotted a platoon of real soldiers and tried to ask them the way. But they were fast marching – sort of jogging down the middle of the road with packs on their backs – and were not allowed to stop. So I had to run backwards down the road for about a quarter of a mile with them, while the sergeant gave me these complicated directions.

Fortunately, when I did meet up with David Croft we got on very well, so I suppose that backward run towards a very tiny role in *It Ain't Half Hot Mum* set me on the way to *'Allo 'Allo*.

Chapter Seventeen

Good Moaning Paris

In May 1989, I took a trip to Paris that I would never have expected to make. It was to launch *'Allo 'Allo* on French TV. To the surprise of all of us involved in the show, except probably David Croft, who seems to take everything in his stride, France's Canal Plus TV station had bought all fifty-six programmes completed at that time.

The purchase followed two years of negotiations and something of a personal crusade on the part of Canal Plus executive Anat Birnbaum, who says she fell in love with the show as soon as she saw it. Anat spotted a group of British TV people roaring with laughter as they gathered around a television set at an international programme-buying conference. She joined them to see what was causing such amusement – and so caught her first glimpse of the antics of René and the gang. Anat, I am glad to say, thought our show was hilarious and set about convincing the bosses of her pay TV channel that it could work in France, too. I understand that not everybody was as enthusiastic as Anat to start with – but she had her way and, incredibly I think, the programme was shown five nights a week in France throughout the summer of 1989.

And although it was transmitted on a pay channel, *'Allo 'Allo* went out to a wider audience than usual because it was used as a come-on for the evening's shows. Canal Plus's programmes are scrambled so that only subscribers can watch – but at the beginning of every evening they broadcast just one of their shows unscrambled in a bid to attract more viewers. And throughout the summer that show was *'Allo 'Allo*.

Canal Plus launched the series in France with a special lunch at a Paris café which they thought was not unlike the Café René. And so on Tuesday, 23 May, Carmen Silvera and I gathered with representatives of Canal Plus, French and visiting British press at the Brasserie du Pont Louis-Philippe on the banks of the Seine. The sun shone warmly upon us and we all tucked in to a French café-style feast of rough country pâté, lentil salad, jellied cold beef, salad, a selection of cheeses and a delicious choice of desserts. Food is a passion of mine, and one of the things I like best about France. I'm not so keen on the wine as most people, but I love the cooking – particularly the peasant style. The Cordon Bleu sort is a little too grand for me, and I find there is something almost obscene in paying £100 or that kind of ridiculous amount for a portion of foie gras. But I am sure I would have enjoyed the kind of food a real-life René would have served up, wartime rations permitting.

Over lunch Anat Birnbaum told me: 'If the French do not laugh at your show I shall have to leave the country.' And French actress Annick Alane, who dubs Carmen's voice, was a little more serious. She told Carmen and me: 'If France does not find *'Allo 'Allo* funny, then I fear for the future of Europe.'

We also met Pierre Tournade, who dubs René. He is a character actor quite well known in France, with a career not unlike mine before *'Allo 'Allo*, and, oddly enough, people tell me he looks not unlike me too. He does not sound like me, though, and I must admit it was very strange for me to listen to Pierre's voice coming out of René's mouth. A Belgian journalist once told me: 'You *are* René.' And I replied, 'Yes, I am René because I am the only one who has ever played him.' He is not exactly Hamlet – who has been portrayed by thousands of actors. The old feller has more than one voice nowadays, though.

French is actually the sixth language into which the show has been dubbed. European audiences have already watched us in Spanish, Italian and the Spanish regional languages of Catalan, Galician and Basque. I felt at first that I would have preferred sub-titles, because I feel that with dubbing you can lose some of the niceties of humour and expression, but the French are among those who have chosen to dub the show. And although my French is not good enough for me really to judge for myself, I am told it works very well. René speaks perfectly ordinary French, and it is just the English who have funny accents. They just speak appalling French with strong English accents. And Crabtree makes the same kind of blunders of pronunciation that he does in our version – only he is speaking French. 'Good moaning' and 'Pissing the café', and all his other gems, will be translated into something which sounds equally funny and incomprehensible in the French language.

It has been reported that the jokes about collaboration between the French and the Nazis have been cut out, but that is not the case. Anyone who has watched the show would know that would not be possible – you would lose just about the whole programme. But the scripts have been restructured and some of the jokes changed, simply because they did not work when translated. The English airmen say 'Cuckoo' instead of 'How do you do', which I do not really understand – nor have I yet found anyone who can explain it to me satisfactorily. But that in itself makes me laugh, and the general French reaction seems very good so far.

'The rest of Europe has split its sides over *'Allo 'Allo*,' reported the television magazine *Télé Poche*. 'But you can understand why there has been reticence about showing it here.' The magazine went on to say: 'The scripts have been superbly rewritten.' And another Paris magazine, *Télé Loisir*, commented: 'This typically British satire doesn't spare anyone.' It asked the question, however: 'Will France appreciate it?'. Anat Birnbaum never had any doubts. 'Of course French audiences will enjoy it,' she said right at the start. 'And we've taken great care to preserve the comedy of character and language which has made *'Allo 'Allo* such a huge hit internationally.'

When Carmen and I flew over to Paris for the launch party we had quite a day, as the show was still running at the Palladium. We left on an early flight and were due to return on a 4.30 flight to Heathrow. It transpired that not only was there a rail strike in London that day, but there was also a transport dispute in Paris. The traffic hold-ups thus caused, combined with a beat-the-clock dash to stage a photograph by the Eiffel Tower, meant that we were late arriving at Charles de Gaulle Airport. And an immovable Air France official refused to let us on the Heathrow-bound plane – even though the flight was still boarding.

Not best pleased with anyone, we managed to catch another flight to Gatwick Airport, battled through the strike-bound traffic into central London, and arrived at the theatre just as the panic was really setting in and everybody was convinced we were not going to make it. No doubt if we appeared in a top-rating American TV show that sold worldwide, it would all be private jets and limousines and helicopters. The BBC does not operate quite like that.

I am fortunate, of course, with my costume – as long as I wear a white shirt and dark trousers, all I need is an apron and a waistcoat. But Carmen had obligingly taken her Edith dress to Paris and nobody had even laid on somewhere for her to change. She struggled into her costume in a tiny room next to the ladies in the café just in time, before Madame the proprietress informed her the room was private. And on the way home she changed in the loo on the aircraft. Can you imagine Joan Collins going through all that?

But we made it back home somehow. The show must and did go on. And we left behind us possibly the most unlikely TV series ever to be seen in France. It was scheduled so that it ran on French TV over Bastille Day on 14 July – the 200th anniversary of the French Revolution – and that same week I was called in by BBC Radio Two to stand in for Ken Bruce on his morning show. I think they thought it was an appropriate time to give René an airing.

René has yet to be invited on to French Radio as a celebrity guest. But who knows? David Croft remains convinced that one day *'Allo 'Allo* will be shown in Germany. I remain sceptical about that but meanwhile we keep plugging on doing our bit for European unity.

Chapter Eighteen

Threatened by Scandal

Introduced by Hilary Bonner.   On Saturday, 21 January 1989 I wrote a feature in the *Daily Mirror* which began:

Gorden Kaye is a gentle, kindly man who happens to be a homosexual. And yesterday he believed that his world lay in ruins.

It was bleakly obvious that he had spent a long and sleepless night. The eyes were tired and sad. The hands shook a little as he fidgeted nervously with his packet of cigarettes.

Only the day before we talked, he learned that lurid details of his secret gay sex life were about to be exposed.

Almost uncomprehending Gorden told me of the anguish he feels. The forty-eight-year-old actor is shy and unassuming, in spite of his huge success as café owner René in *'Allo 'Allo*. And he did not sound like a big TV star when he told me just why he had turned to rent boys.

'I do not think I am terribly attractive, you see,' he said. 'I know I have a good personality. But when you are balding and overweight and in your forties, then you are not likely to find yourself someone who is young and attractive. So I have been to male prostitutes. There was a club in London that I used to go to about eighteen months ago where I met rent boys – but only three or four times. I realize now that it was a silly thing to do.'

My story appeared on the front page, and it was made clear that we were printing it on Gorden's request and because he feared that a rent boy he was once involved with was going to make allegations about him in a Sunday newspaper.

Gorden answered all my questions honestly. He did not ask to see and approve my copy. He has since been generous in his praise of the way the *Daily Mirror* handled the story. He believes that we were both sympathetic and truthful, and that we turned a time bomb which he felt could wreck his career into a damp squib. And we received hundreds of letters from *Daily Mirror* readers both supporting Gorden and praising the *Mirror*'s coverage.

It is of course no longer against the law to be homosexual in this country. But sometimes it seems that nothing much has changed since the days of Oscar Wilde. I was deeply moved when I talked to Gorden before writing the article. Like a criminal he was in hiding, for goodness sake, at the house of some friends in South London. He had asked me not to reveal the secret address to anybody else, and in order not to break that confidence I had installed our photographer Bill Rowntree in a pub down the road, where Gorden and I later met up with him. The whole thing was quite ridiculous when you think about it. It is easy nowadays to take the common way out – blaming those sections of the media which encourage the prejudice against homosexuality that continues to flourish – but it is not just the press which has created that prejudice. It breeds in almost every bar-room and in every office block and on every shop floor, and I do not think any honest man or woman could deny that.

At the time Gorden said: 'I do not feel I have done anything wrong, you see. I know some people will not agree, but for myself that is how I see it. I am not a bad person. I have never corrupted anybody. I have never forced my attentions on anybody. I am not that kind of homosexual. I have never knowingly been with anyone under twenty-one. I am not that kind of homosexual either. I do not wander the streets picking men up. I am not even particularly highly-sexed. I am not at it like a rabbit every night. Far from it. But yes, I am gay.'

And I wrote in that feature article: 'Gorden Kaye is a homely type, fond of comfortable sweaters and slippers. By temperament he is ideally suited to conventional marriage. It is his private tragedy that his sexuality will bar him from that for ever.'

Of all that I wrote about Gorden Kaye at this tormented time when he felt forced publicly to reveal aspects of his life which he considered to be totally private, that was the only sentence to which he took exception. 'Being gay is not a tragedy,' he told me reprovingly.

He knows, however, that that was not in fact the suggestion. I stand by what I was trying to put across – that apart from the tiresome matter of sex, Gorden really would be an ideal husband. He would like nothing better than to be a family man – and it is a personal tragedy, I believe, that he is denied this.

Most of this book is full of fun and of razzmatazz and tells the behind the scenes story of a great comedy programme and a highly talented comedy actor. For me it has a more serious side. And that is to present Gorden Kaye as the thoroughly decent, likeable chap that he is. A loyal friend. An entertaining companion. A loving son intensely fond of all his surviving family. A man whose homosexuality is just a part of him.

It is insulting to the man, really, to point out that his partners have always been consenting grown-up people with minds of their own. His sex life, I should imagine, is much the same as that of most of us – largely uneventful, and punctuated by moments of abandoned passion, sometimes very lovely and sometimes best forgotten. That he should actually fear that his career might end – as an actor, too, not a member of government or a bishop – because of an indeed ill-advised carnal act with another willing adult is, in 1989, a bit silly.

My involvement with the rent boy story Gorden so feared, began when the showbusiness lawyer Oscar Beuselink, called in by the producers of the Palladium *'Allo 'Allo* show to advise Gorden on what action he should take, contacted Ernie Burrington, deputy chairman of Mirror Group newspapers, on the morning of Friday, 20 January 1989. He told him that a scandal was about to break concerning Gorden Kaye, which Gorden would like to discuss with the *Daily Mirror* first because he believed that newspaper would present the facts more fairly. I was duly

summoned to the office of the editor, Richard Stott, at around
11 a.m.

We did not know what form the scandalous story was going to
take, only that it concerned Gorden's sexuality, which was not
then public knowledge, and that Gorden believed that certain
Sunday newspapers were about to print articles which might be
damaging to him. I was given a secret telephone number where I
could contact Gorden, and arranged to meet him as soon as possible
at his hideaway address. I told him I could only help him if he was
prepared to tell the truth, and he assured me that, having made
the decision to take this course of action and to talk to me, he
would not dream of doing anything else.

By this time I was in something of a dilemma myself. I had,
ironically, always tried to avoid covering routine *'Allo 'Allo* stories
for the *Mirror* because he and I lived so close to each other.
And so on this grey Friday morning I could quite selfishly see the
obvious dangers threatening my own private life if things did not
turn out the way Gorden was hoping. I imagined for evermore
having to dodge him when I popped out to collect the milk, and I
considered trying to arrange for someone else to talk to him.
Ultimately I decided that I had no real choice, that I must
do the job myself, and so I drove to South London for a very
harrowing interview.

As we put the story together at the *Mirror* office in Holborn
Circus our competitors began to suspect that Gorden had told us
all. Indeed he and Oscar Beuselink, I later learned, answered all
inquiries that Friday with the statement that Gorden had said
everything he intended to say to another national newspaper.

I received two phone calls during the course of the afternoon,
allegedly from the *Daily Mirror*'s legal department asking to check
certain facts in my story. The first I referred to the editor – to the
persistent irritation of the caller. Under pressure to meet a tight
deadline I did not give much thought to the authenticity of the call,
but by the time my secretary received the second one, which I was
genuinely too busy to take, I had grave suspicions. Several months
later a rather tired and emotional executive of a rival newspaper
told me with some pride at a Fleet Street party that, as I had indeed

suspected, a senior journalist on his paper had made the calls in an attempt to trick me into revealing details of our story. The trick did not work.

And for Gorden the purpose of his admission to the *Daily Mirror* was achieved. His homosexuality became public knowledge in a straightforward and honest way, and hopefully no longer presents a threat. But at the same time the situation was alarming, and only Gorden can describe what it actually felt like for him. . . .

*   *   *

At 5.30 in the evening of Saturday, 20 January I stood at the top of the stairs, backstage at the London Palladium, waiting for the curtain to go up and wondering just what sort of reception I would get after the revelations that morning about my sex life. The curtain rose and the ceiling lifted. Standing there in René's apron and waistcoat before a roaring audience of 2300, I had no doubt that their enthusiastic reception was specially for me on this very difficult day. Our show is popular and we are used to applause. But nothing like this. The people in our audience that afternoon probably have no idea how much it meant to me.

There is still great prejudice towards homosexuality in this country, not least in certain areas of the press, and I honestly believed that I stood to lose everything I had achieved after I was forced to reveal that I was gay and that I had been with rent boys. To me that audience reaction was the first clear indication that I would survive after all. In my own eyes I had done nothing really wrong, although I had behaved stupidly. But I had laid myself open to the kind of scandal which can still bring a celebrity down.

A couple of years previously, while working very hard on the stage show of *'Allo 'Allo* when it first opened in the West End at the Prince of Wales Theatre, I took to going late at night to a couple of Soho bars at which many of the customers were gay. I had never experienced theatre at that level and pace before. *'Allo 'Allo* is a two-hour show and I am on stage for all but eleven minutes. Do not misunderstand me – I find it quite exhilarating and I love every minute of it. I would much rather be up there in the thick of it than sitting bored in my dressing room, waiting for my next call. But it does mean that, particularly in the beginning, I was inclined to come off stage with the adrenalin still pumping frantically and looking for something to do, people to be with. Perhaps, if I am honest, looking for some more excitement.

I live alone – as I have explained before, I have not been lucky enough to find that special someone with whom to share my life. I have many friends, including just a few very close ones whom I treasure greatly, but they are not always available to provide companionship in the middle of the night for a hyperactive actor. And so it was largely in search of company that I went on no more than a handful of times to these bars. But on two or three occasions I met young men there whom I found attractive, and whom it transpired were male prostitutes – rent boys as they are known. They were available and I was alone, and arrangements were made.

It is not something I am proud of, and certainly not something I would ever have spoken about in public had I not more or less been forced to do so, in order to protect myself from lies which I had reason to believe were about to be told. Looking back, I was certainly misguided, and had also totally overlooked just how well known I had become.

At least one of these young men, I understand, was preparing to sell his story to the highest bidder in Fleet Street. I was devastated when I found out, not least because I do not actually consider that what I did was anybody else's business. It was a period of uncertain behaviour in my life which I do not think I would have repeated even if the events of January 1989 had not occurred. What I did was actually out of character for me because I am not a man with a love of glitzy parties or nightclubs – and loneliness was a factor. Given a choice I would much prefer a quiet dinner with friends after working in the theatre, and quite often I simply go home alone to watch television – from videos I have recorded – for a couple of hours to wind down.

Thursday, 19 January started out like any other day, as they say in all the worst movies. I arrived at the Palladium at twenty past six in the evening, made myself a cup of coffee and sat down to watch some television and answer some of the fan mail that had collected that day.

At about 6.45 the stage doorkeeper called to say that a reporter from the *People* newspaper wanted a word with me. This was an unexpected visit which had not been arranged through our Press Office, so I told the stage doorman to tell him to contact our publicity people. The message came back that the visit concerned a rather delicate matter and that the reporter would like to speak to me directly for just a couple of minutes, if possible.

I relented, and was told by the representative of the *People* that he had some disturbing news to relay to me. The *News of the World* was about to release a rather sleazy exposé of my private life, for which they had signed affidavits from a number of rent boys I was alleged to have associated with, and some photographs. He told me I had been followed for some months in order that this exposé could be put together. The *People*, I was told, would be prepared to print what he called a 'spoiler' article.

I was absolutely stunned. I made no comment, concluded the interview and immediately contacted my producer, Mark Furness, who put me in touch with Oscar Beuselink. He indeed advised me to go for a 'spoiler' article, but we chose to turn to Hilary Bonner and to the *Daily Mirror*, and indeed the way that newspaper handled the affair confirmed that we had made absolutely the right decision. The *Daily Mirror* behaved honourably and told the truth without undue sensationalism, and indeed in a far more sympathetic manner than I had dared to expect. The situation was defused to a considerable extent.

But my ordeal was not over. Representatives of several newspapers pursued me over that weekend, including a *News of the World* reporter who told me in writing that her newspaper had never intended to write an exposé of my sex life, that they did not have the relevant information, that it was in fact another newspaper that had been following me for months and that, in their words: 'You have been stitched up.'

I suggested to the *News of the World* that that should then be their story, but they chose instead to print an article that was not based on a proper interview with me. Among other things it contained the comment by Mr Geoffrey Dickens MP that, because of the revelations about my private life, I should resign immediately from playing René in *'Allo 'Allo*, 'since this is good family entertainment, and people are never going to watch the show in the same light again'.

To my great satisfaction, the following Wednesday Jean Rook wrote in her column in the *Daily Express*:

That 18 stone monolith of public morals Mr Dickens – more famed for drinking tea than Parisian plonk – might recall that he has had his own slips betwixt teacup and lip.

The roly-poly politician's penchant for afternoon dances in Tea Emporiums temporarily dried up his marriage – and would have ended it had not his wife, Norma, poured forgiveness on Geoffrey's publicly-shed remorse.

Since that time he's never splashed a drop of the milk of human tolerance in anybody's tea but his own. Having seen the light, Mr Dickens is permanently bathed in it, and fattened with all the smugness of the reformed Prodigal.

I suspect he spends weekends behind the spotless picture windows of his Saddleworth, near Manchester, mansion, selecting stones to hurl.

Like the Good Moaning Gendarme who pips in for a drunk, the self-righteous Mr Dickens speaks a different language from the rest of us.

I believe that the millions who've drunk hours of pleasure from René's Café will still frequent it.

So that effectively answered that one, and called for no further reaction from me.

The *News of the World* had meanwhile launched a readers' phone-in asking whether I should resign or not. I named it the Nuremberg phone-in. The *News of the World* readers apparently voted something like ten to one in favour of my staying on as René, and about mid-week I was asked by the newspaper if I would like to thank their readers who were so obviously my fans. I was more than happy to do just that.

I am still unclear which papers had exactly what information and who planned to print what. I do not care very much, and in any case the strange thing is that in the end a lot of good came out of my being forced to make the admissions I did. Perhaps because of my conventional working-class Yorkshire upbringing I had always had a terrific fear of my homosexuality becoming public knowledge.

There are a great many gay people in the showbusiness world, and I am fortunate to have become part of a society where my sexuality has never been a problem. I am sure that everyone I work with, and certainly most of my friends, had always been aware of the nature of my sexuality. Ironically, I am told that most of Fleet Street always knew too.

But it was an entirely different thing for me to have to face the general public with this revelation. As I told the *Daily Mirror* in January, about a couple of years earlier I had been talking to a friend and I had said that if my 'secret' were ever to be revealed, I would top myself. In the event it never crossed my mind. Somehow I faced up to it. And as things turned out, I think I worried too much. There is no doubt that a weight has been lifted from my mind, because I really did fear for my future. I thought it was quite possible that the BBC might begin to phase me out – after all, apart from anything else, in René I do play the part of a quite definitely heterosexual married man who indulges in frequent slap and tickle with one of his waitresses, and is always dodging the unwelcome advances of a gay Nazi officer.

But among the first expressions of support I received, was an assertion from the BBC that not only was there no question of my being phased out, but this had never been considered.

On the eve of the publication of the *Daily Mirror* article I contacted my family and made sure that the production team and all the cast and backroom people at the Palladium knew what was about to happen. I apologized for any discomfort which they might be caused. Once again the support was unanimous and very heartwarming.

On the Saturday the article was published, I arrived at the theatre to find my dressing room full of flowers, and messages and letters of support were already beginning to flood in. I received more than seven hundred letters in all – some arrived at the BBC, some at the Palladium and some were sent to the *Daily Mirror*. A number were from people who did not approve of homosexuality, often on religious grounds, but all, apart from one, mightily defended my right to privacy in my personal life and to behave sexually according to my own standards and not anybody else's. I can honestly say that only one was not supportive, and I replied to that one as well as to the others.

I tried to respond personally to all the letters – although some clearly said they did not want a reply and others had no address on them. If I missed out anyone who felt they should have had a reply I would like to take this opportunity now to thank all the well-wishers. They gave me tremendous support at a time when it was much needed.

'Thank you for the pleasure you have given me with your performances – you are a very gifted actor who must rise above all this,' was a fairly typical message. 'All my family love you and your acting gives us much pleasure. What you do in your private life is nothing to do with anyone else. Just keep up the good work,' read one letter. And I received another very moving one from a lady who said that her brother had just died, and on his very last evening they had sat together and laughed over *'Allo 'Allo*. She said the programme and René had meant so much to them both that she wanted to write to me and give her support – and incredibly she wrote that letter just two days after her brother died.

I discovered through what was probably the worst forty-eight hours of my life that I am a much luckier man than I realized. I do not have so much to fear after all.

I have been blessed with the gift of being funny. I can make people laugh – and I had not realized how much one can be loved just for that. My family and friends appear wonderfully unshaken to learn that I am gay – and in the end that is truly all that matters.

I have not taken to launching myself on a wild round of night-clubbing, now that my behaviour would probably no longer be newsworthy. In fact just the opposite. My private life continues much the same as it was before – by and large very quietly. My pleasures are those of a home-loving man. I like to read and listen to music and to watch television. I am not the gifted gardener my father was, but I gain great satisfaction from my small terrace garden overlooking the Thames. I greatly enjoy travel, and elsewhere in this book there are a number of stories about holidays and other trips I have taken.

I have not taken these revelations about myself as an opportunity to let my hair down and be outrageous or flamboyant or 'theatrical' in any way. Nothing has changed, except that I no longer feel I have a secret to keep, and that is a relief.

Chapter Nineteen

Banana on the Lawn

It is by now no secret that *'Allo 'Allo* has quite a bit in common with the classic BBC TV drama series, *Secret Army*. So it was with some trepidation that I set out for Bournemouth in the summer of 1983, to begin filming an adaptation of *Mansfield Park* by Jane Austen. If there seems to be no logic in that last sentence I would add that one of the principal actors in *Mansfield Park* was Bernard Hepton who, to all intents and purposes, played the parallel role to René – Albert – in *Secret Army*.

Although at that time we had only filmed the pilot episode, it had been shown twice, and I was sure I was going to get the cold shoulder from Mr Hepton for poking fun at his marvellous creation. I worried needlessly. When I tentatively broached the subject he hadn't even heard of *'Allo 'Allo*, but said it sounded like fun. I gather that he caught up with it subsequently and enjoyed it. Coincidentally both his Belgian Albert and my French René are Yorkshiremen underneath. He is from Bradford and I, of course, am from Huddersfield, and we each worked for a time as amateurs at the Bradford Playhouse Theatre.

It was while making *Mansfield Park* that I came across a strange semi-technical phrase which stuck in mind to such an extent that I promised myself that if ever I *did* do an autobiography I would use it for the title. But that of course was before *'Allo 'Allo*.

I was shooting a scene with Sylvestra Le Touzel. She was in the foreground of the frame sheltering from a rainstorm under a tree at the front gate of the parsonage. The door of the parsonage was some 150 feet behind her, and the shot called for me to come out of the house with an umbrella and walk down across a lawn to collect Sylvestra and take her into the house. As usual when the script demands rain it was a hot sunny day, and the local fire brigade were on hand to provide a downpour.

We rehearsed, and I ran towards the camera and my fellow actor. Apparently, for most of the journey I had placed myself immediately behind Sylvestra and so could not be seen approaching her. The first assistant was sent to me with a memorable message from the director, David Giles. 'David says can you do a banana on the lawn?' he said.

In case this is not entirely clear – as indeed at the time it was not to me – I should point out that there are occasions when moving in a straight line either directly towards the lens, as in this instance, or across the frame close to the camera, can screw up the shot. It is necessary then to take a curved path, hence the strange expression which tickled my imagination. So you might be reading a book called *A Banana on the Lawn* had René Artois not felt he had some part in my life story.

The filming of *Mansfield Park* took sixteen weeks. I worked for four weeks, had two weeks off, and then worked on and off for the remaining ten. I had bought myself a portable video recorder, and as we were on location I managed to compile a few bits for a half-hour 'end of term' video.

Breakfast Television had just got going, and so, using bits recorded during breaks in filming and specially written sequences, a one-off programme called *Good Morning Mansfield* was concocted. Amongst the items was a keep-fit session. Leslie Crowther's daughter Liz was in the series, playing the role of Julia Bertram, so it was called *Julia's Jerks*. (Actually it was called *Jerk-off with Julia*, but this is a book for the whole family.) I played Dr Grant, a country parson, and Sue Edmonstone was Mrs Grant. We didn't have christian names, so in our little TV send-up we became Kevin and Tracey Grant. And our son Mr Rushwork Grant did the horoscopes.

I managed to acquire some out-takes – not even transmittable on *It'll Be All Right on the Night* – and a helpful BBC technician facilitated captions and a music track, as well as the dialogue. Incidentally, no licence payers' money was used in the making of this programme – so don't write in.

Also while filming *Mansfield Park* we would have nightly rounds of a wonderful game called Couples. Basically you put the most unlikely people with the same surname together as couples – Kenneth and Esther Williams, Roy and Ginger Rogers, Sir John and Mrs Mills, and so on. It is a great game to play if you are stuck in a traffic jam too.

Mansfield Park was probably the last major production I worked on, before *'Allo 'Allo* so thoroughly took over my working life. One of the great moments of *'Allo 'Allo* for me was our successful tour of New Zealand, at the end of 1988, immediately prior to opening at the Palladium. It was a fabulous experience, made particularly special because I had so many new relatives to discover there. One night in Auckland they gave a party for me, and everybody had to wear name tags so that I would know who they all were.

New Zealand is like Britain was twenty-five years ago – loads of old British cars, a super climate, breathtaking scenery, and people with time to stop and look around and enjoy themselves. In 1990, when we take the stage show to Australia, I shall eagerly return for a holiday.

Travel is a passion of mine and I am particularly fortunate to have been able to travel so much with my work. But flying is not a favourite pastime. On my flight home from New Zealand at the beginning of December, I wondered if the Palladium show might not happen after all – not for me, anyway. I always watch the 'No Smoking' sign avidly, not just because I invariably want a cigarette, but also because I know I can relax when it goes off after take-off.

On this occasion, flying out of Kuala Lumpur there was a lurch and a vibration when we left the runway. I stared anxiously at the 'No Smoking' sign which stayed resolutely lit as we held level flight not far above the ground. For fifteen minutes we waited, tension mounting. Finally the captain came on the intercom and said:

'Ladies and gentlemen, this is the captain. I have some bad news', which was not the kind of remark designed to comfort the nervous. Strangely, although I could see the chances of my Palladium début receding dramatically behind the horizon, and clearly visualize the headlines proclaiming 'TV actor perishes aboard London-bound jet', I actually felt strangely resigned and calm.

As it happened it was a faulty engine, and Boeing thoughtfully provide three more on their 747s. So after dumping fuel we were back on the ground in an hour – and another hour after that were installed overnight in a hotel in downtown Kuala Lumpur.

I remember once flying with TWA across the USA from Boston to Los Angeles, and the man in the next aisle seat had downed a fair quantity of strong liquor and was getting a bit stroppy. As the stewardess served the meals he gazed in a bleary-eyed way at her totally non-committal expression. 'Smile!' he demanded.

'I will if you will,' said the girl.

The passenger gave a broad leering grin. 'Now hold that for five hours,' ordered the stewardess as she backed her trolley up the aisle.

Americans have already charmed me with their wit and laconic delivery. On a visit to Las Vegas, I stepped from the air-conditioned plane on to the runway which was like an oven, then back into the relief of more air conditioning in the airport centre, staggered wilting across an arid pavement, stepped into an air-conditioned cab, and duly arrived at my 'climate-controlled' hotel. It was a stifling 117 degrees outside, and as I checked in I made a typically British remark to the receptionist. 'Phew, what a scorcher' (or something very like), I said. 'What did people do here before air conditioning?'

'Most of 'em died,' he replied bleakly.

Another time in St Louis, while touring with *As You Like It*, I was asked by the manager if everything was satisfactory with my room. I hesitated, but he seemed eager to please, so I said: 'Everything is fine, but actually there is a little scrap of paper on the floor of my room which has been there since I arrived. Perhaps the chambermaid is not doing her job too well.'

He looked aghast, pressed a hidden button by his desk, and from a side door emerged a large black lady looking like Mike Tyson in a frock. 'Yeah?' she growled.

'Beryl, this gentleman is in Room 504, and he tells me that there has been a scrap of paper on the floor of his room for the past five days,' said the manager accusingly.

Beryl looked at him, looked at me, looked back at him.

'Why don't he pick it up?' she said, and exited whence she had come.

I could think of no answer to that. Why indeed did I not pick it up?

New York also took a bit of getting used to. It is such a tough city. Whenever I go there I think of the actor who went to New York for a week to make a commercial. His wife was very frightened of the city and told him to be sure never to go out on his own at night. But after four days of eating in the hotel dining room every evening and then going to his room to watch television, he decided he would just take a walk around the block.

Within minutes of leaving the hotel a fairly undesirable-looking character bumped into him, apologized and walked on. The actor checked his jacket pocket and found that his wallet was missing. He ran after the man who had bumped into him, threw him against a wall and yelled: 'Give me the wallet. Just give me the wallet.' The terrified man did as he was told, and our actor returned to his hotel room to find his own wallet lying on the bed where he had put it before leaving the room. Four days in New York and he had become a mugger. America is quite a country, and whatever the future holds for me, I am determined it will involve a great deal of travel and many trips across the Atlantic.

My home now overlooks the Thames in West London, and it is the second home that I have owned. I bought my first place, a flat in Whitton, soon after moving South in 1979 and when I had made a little money from *Born and Bred*. My home life is important to me, but as I have said before, I live alone and my work is inclined to come first. I never seem to have had a relationship and a good job at the same time. I don't know why. I have had nice relationships with people and not much work going on, and then

I have had good jobs and nobody in my life. If I could ever get the two together I would be a happy man.

Since the beginning of *'Allo 'Allo*, everything that I have done has revolved around that show, and I know that goes for most of the rest of the cast too. Sadly, two of our most loved performers, Sam Kelly and Jack Haig, had to leave us due to ill health. Sam Kelly and I worked together years ago in Sheffield on a favourite play of mine called *Black Comedy* which, curiously enough, relied entirely upon the principle of illusion we use in *'Allo 'Allo*. We make the audience believe that René is speaking French while Crabtree is speaking appalling French, and Michelle is usually speaking French until she adopts an exaggerated Oxford accent when she is speaking English. In fact everybody is, of course, speaking English with various funny accents, but if you do something of this sort with enough care and seriousness you will take an audience with you – as *'Allo 'Allo* has proved.

Black Comedy is based on the old Chinese theatrical illusion of light reversal. The show starts off in total blackness – the curtain goes up and everything is black. The audience becomes aware that there are two people on stage. One says: 'Oh, what a lovely flat. Shall I put a record on?'

The other replies: 'Yes, darling. Would you like a drink?'

The music starts to play and the audience are wondering what on earth is going on. Suddenly there is a bang, the record player whines to a halt, the lights come on, and the lady on stage says: 'Blast. A fuse has gone.'

From then on the stage is in full light but the cast blunder around as if they are in the dark. The audience has to accept that they cannot see where they are going, and the play is about the mayhem that ensues. There is a scene where Sam Kelly has to move furniture in the dark, and he is crawling on his knees groping for the door with his arm straight out in front of him. He is heading directly towards my crutch and I am flapping my jacket to make myself even more vulnerable to this hand that is about to grab me. At the last moment he turns away.

The audience gasp, and I remember people being so convinced it was pitch black they would ask Sam: 'How on earth did you manage to do that at just the right time?' He would say: 'Because I can bloody see, of course.' But the whole crux of the play was to suspend the audience's disbelief. And that is how the language thing works in *'Allo 'Allo*.

The late and much missed Jack Haig, of course, seemed to have been in showbusiness for ever, and was a very clever stand-up comic who specialized in biting one-liners off stage as well as on. Most were unprintable, but I remember an exchange between us which was particularly funny coming from a comedian. It concerned a scene in the stage show where Jack's character, LeClerc, gave me a stuffed parrot in which was concealed a radio transmitter. The microphone was in the bird's beak and the controls were at the other end. Naturally, to operate this transmitter I had to press the parrot's parson's nose, and Jack Haig as LeClerc told me that when I did so the parrot's beak would open.

René replied: 'I am not surprised,' and the audience always roared with laughter.

Originally they would also laugh as soon as the parrot appeared, and Jack took to banging his fist on the counter, effectively killing the earlier laugh. That way, he claimed, I got a bigger laugh for the punchline, and I argued against this on the basis that it is always good to have an audience laughing and we shouldn't ever stop them.

Jack shook his head sorrowfully and said: 'You youngsters. I've been killing laughs for sixty years.'

He actually celebrated his seventy-sixth birthday on stage at the Palladium in January 1989. Just before the appropriate show he popped into my dressing room and casually dropped into the conversation that today was his birthday.

I glossed over it, and he was quite persistent, so eventually I said obliquely: 'Oh yes, mine's in April.'

Of course we had all known for days, and we also knew that, like everybody in the show and in spite of all his years in the business, he had never before worked the Palladium, that most famous and cherished of variety theatres, and he was overjoyed to be there.

As we took our final bows that night René stopped the audience's applause and demanded that they join the cast in a 2300-voice rendition of 'Happy Birthday' for Jack. Moved and thrilled to bits, he ran along the edge of the stage, shaking hands with the front row customers. His untimely death in July 1989 has left a hole in the *'Allo 'Allo* family – it's like losing a favourite uncle. He will be missed by colleagues and the public alike. It is a fitting tribute that his last job should be at the Palladium, a theatre venerated by performers throughout the world.

Chapter Twenty

'Allo 'Allo and Onward

'Universally loved by the public, universally panned by the critics.' That is my standard quote when asked about reaction to the stage show of *'Allo 'Allo*. The show was a huge hit at the London Palladium, where it was brought in just before Christmas 1988 to fill the gap left by the collapse of the multi million-pound Harold Fielding musical, *Ziegfeld*.

'Allo 'Allo, the last-minute stand-in, with many of its cast committed elsewhere, smashed all records at the Palladium for a non-musical and did such consistent big business that its run was extended by nine weeks. Every week it was among London's top ten West End shows, and usually in the top three or four – in one week alone it grossed £300,000.

I had to negotiate to be excused from my contract for my next project, a comedy play called *Elsie and Norm's Macbeth* co-starring Madge Hindle. The production's national tour has been delayed from the spring to the autumn of 1989. Carmen Silvera was contracted to play pantomime at Southampton, and her agent and the *'Allo 'Allo* producers indulged in complex and expensive negotiations to free her.

The show opened at the Palladium to record-breaking advance bookings of £1½ million. In 1986 it grossed a £500,000 advance booking bonanza for its West End début at the Prince of Wales Theatre – way beyond expectations – and continued to be a sell-out throughout its run there. Earlier, at its provincial opening in

Birmingham, advance bookings again broke the theatre's records, the fans queued for returns, and one woman laughed so much she passed out and an ambulance had to be called. And when *'Allo 'Allo* toured New Zealand for six weeks in the autumn of 1988, the show took in excess of two million New Zealand dollars at the box office, and became one of the most successful touring productions in that country's history.

Certain London critics must be spitting blood. When *'Allo 'Allo* opened at the Prince of Wales, later to become the home of Andrew Lloyd Webber's *Aspects of Love*, Kenneth Hurren of the *Mail on Sunday* described it as 'vulgar and witless'. Milton Shulman of the *London Evening Standard* referred to 'characters I find about as funny as pall-bearers in the rain'. And the show's cruellest critic of all, the *Daily Mail's* Jack Tinker, stormed: ''*Allo 'Allo* is Bye Bye to the theatre as we know it. . . .

'My own anger is reserved for the fact that, lured by their devotion to the series on TV, their fans are going to flock to the Prince of Wales and go away thinking they have been to the theatre. Nothing could be further from the truth.'

Strangely, although I can sometimes still be extremely unsure of myself and nervous when I walk out on to a stage, the critics never worried me. We knew they wouldn't like us. We knew they would treat us as if we were Chekhov – and that is ridiculous. They say *'Allo 'Allo* is not art. But if it is not art to entertain people as much as we do, I don't know what is.

Producer Mark Furness was not worried either. 'We knew we had a winner,' he said.

Alex Renton of the *Independent* reviewed the show when it returned to the West End at the London Palladium. He didn't like it but recognized that everyone else in the theatre most certainly did. He wrote: 'It is sad to be the only person in a packed theatre not having the time of their life, so I made an effort to try to like some of the characters.' That is the sort of review I can accept. And he was very kind about me. 'Gorden Kaye's René, selfish, glum and fatalistic, is a comic creation of some class – an anti-hero who wants nothing more out of the war than to survive,' he said.

In any case, both in the theatre and at home in front of the television set, all the show's fans have demonstrated splendid disregard for the critics. Ninety million people now watch 'Allo 'Allo on television throughout the world. They have displayed their loyalty at the Prince of Wales, at the Palladium – probably the greatest variety theatre in history – and at more than 680 sell-out performances nationwide and worldwide.

There are now sixty-four episodes of 'Allo 'Allo in the can – and although it is unlikely that any more will be made during 1990, the BBC plan to repeat the existing shows throughout the year. The TV show, of course, also attracted its share of criticism when it began, notably again from the Daily Mail – in this case its TV critic Herbert Kretzmer, whose comments I have recorded earlier. At the time, this led to a spirited defence of the programme from one of its greatest fans, Terry Wogan, who accused Herbie of having no sense of humour.

Over Christmas 1989, it is hoped to produce the stage show in Brighton. It will tour Australia in the spring of 1990 and probably Scandinavia later in the year, where 'Allo 'Allo is a huge hit on TV.

Of course a top TV comedy show such as ours does not just mean that recognition thing off screen – knowing that if you are in a restaurant there are probably a number of people watching closely to see if you know how to use your knife and fork. It also means for its principal actors massive exposure to the public as one particular character, in my case René Artois. I have already said that I am aware I am very typecast, and I am not sure what will or can come next.

I have always fancied hosting a TV chat show, and perhaps such an opportunity will present itself one day. I would probably be very bad at it, but I would like to have a go. I visualize getting some very disparate guests together and letting them do a bit of hammering out in front of an audience and the TV cameras. It would be a fairly serious show, in which some of the things that irritate us all and affect our lives would be explained and argued through by people who really knew their stuff.

I have this idea, you see, that if I could get the right kind of guest mix, all I would have to do would be to say: 'Good evening. My guests this evening are . . . blah blah.' And then at the end say: 'I hope you enjoyed it. See you next week.' But I suppose if it were that easy anybody could do it.

I should like to return to the theatre more, and maybe even do a pantomime again.

But whatever the future holds, I have a varied past to look back on, and I reckon I have come a long way since days of the Bradford Playhouse. This book has charted that route from rep to René, and some of what happened along the road.

In those car-delivering days we would sometimes hitch lifts back to base, and I remember travelling in a truck carrying six hundred pigeons to France. The driver told me that pigeons will only ever fly in one direction – if you took a group of pigeons which usually fly south, and released them to the south of their destination, they would never find their way home.

I do not know my destination after *'Allo 'Allo*. But, in any event, I have the feeling we have not seen the last of that roguish French café owner. It is not entirely up to me, but I believe René would like Yvette to chase him around the bar a few more times.

I don't think the old lad is quite ready to hang up his apron yet.